Cloud Storage Security

Cloud Storage Security
A Practical Guide

Aaron Wheeler

Michael Winburn

AMSTERDAM • BOSTON • HEIDELBERG • LONDON
NEW YORK • OXFORD • PARIS • SAN DIEGO
SAN FRANCISCO • SINGAPORE • SYDNEY • TOKYO

Elsevier
Radarweg 29, PO Box 211, 1000 AE Amsterdam, Netherlands
The Boulevard, Langford Lane, Kidlington, Oxford OX5 1GB, UK
225 Wyman Street, Waltham, MA 02451, USA

Notices
Knowledge and best practice in this field are constantly changing. As new research and
experience broaden our understanding, changes in research methods, professional practices,
or medical treatment may become necessary.

Practitioners and researchers must always rely on their own experience and knowledge in
evaluating and using any information, methods, compounds, or experiments described herein.
In using such information or methods they should be mindful of their own safety and the safety
of others, including parties for whom they have a professional responsibility.

To the fullest extent of the law, neither the Publisher nor the authors, contributors, or editors,
assume any liability for any injury and/or damage to persons or property as a matter of products
liability, negligence or otherwise, or from any use or operation of any methods, products,
instructions, or ideas contained in the material herein.

ISBN: 978-0-12-802930-5

British Library Cataloguing-in-Publication Data
A catalogue record for this book is available from the British Library

Library of Congress Cataloging-in-Publication Data
A catalog record for this book is available from the Library of Congress

For Information on all Elsevier publications
visit our website at http://store.elsevier.com/

Working together
to grow libraries in
developing countries

www.elsevier.com • www.bookaid.org

CONTENTS

CHAPTER *1*

Data in the Cloud

This chapter introduces cloud storage concepts, puts cloud data privacy and security in an historical context, and identifies privacy and security issues. Subsequent chapters will delve more fully into the details of privacy and security for cloud data storage.

1.1 DEFINITIONS AND HISTORY

1.1.1 Definitions

Before we discuss data in the cloud, we must first define what we mean both by the cloud and by data.

The National Institute of Standards and Technology (NIST) Special Publication 800-145 (NIST SP 800-145) defines the cloud as the hardware and software infrastructure required to provide "on-demand self-service, broad network access, resource pooling, rapid elasticity, and measured service." These characteristics allow for three service models: software, platform, and infrastructure (Mell and Grance, 2011).

Software as a Service (SaaS) gives consumers use of software from providers that runs on cloud infrastructure. Examples of SaaS include social media like Facebook, Twitter, YouTube, and Pinterest. SaaS also includes email, website hosting, and data storage. Platform as a Service (PaaS) enables consumers to deploy and run their own software on the provider's cloud infrastructure. Infrastructure as a Service (IaaS) means cloud providers host customer operating systems, so customers use their own software and control some network components (Mell and Grance, 2011).

NIST recognizes four deployment models for these service models: private, communal, public, or hybrid. Private clouds service a single individual, group, or organization. Communal clouds provide cloud services to a restricted community of consumers. Public clouds provide cloud services to the general public. Hybrid clouds have aspects of the other three, often to optimize these services (Mell and Grance, 2011).

By data we mean digital files like pictures, music, and documents; comments posted in tweets, blogs, and discussion threads. These things constitute data that you consciously place in cloud storage. However, your interaction with your cloud storage also provides or generates additional information, both about you and your data. This information could directly impact your privacy and security, or at a minimum it could leak or reveal important details about data that you thought private and secure. Cloud storage servers routinely collect this metadata, as do web browsers or applications that interact with cloud storage.

Cloud storage providers will collect metadata about your usage patterns, including network IP address, time, file size, file name, file action (add, modify, delete, etc.) to aid in quality of service (QoS).

Cloud data storage has many advantages for people, organizations, and companies. Cloud services give small businesses cost-effective access to capabilities that large companies often handle internally, thus bringing the benefits of scale economies to small businesses and making them more competitive. Cloud service providers also make these capabilities affordable to individuals too. Cloud services benefit people and companies by outsourcing hardware, software, maintenance, and management of data storage. Cloud storage provides off-site backup of critical data and allows access to the data anytime from anywhere. Cloud storage customers can easily increase their storage capacity too. Finally, studies have shown that outsourcing to the cloud can significantly cut company energy costs (Nedbal and Stieninger, 2014).

1.1.2 History

The fundamental capabilities we depend on the Internet for mostly existed from the early days. In some sense, Internet technology innovation has come from finding ways to make the original capabilities more accessible to more people. Cloud computing comes as no exception.

Mainframe computers in use beginning in the 1950s had most of the capabilities we associate with cloud computing: powerful servers providing data storage, software, and processing. By the early 1970s, mainframes had hardware virtualization capabilities (Amrehn and Elliott, 2012). These early mainframes did suffer from limited, non-graphical user interfaces, ranging from punch cards to teletype to keyboards (Bergin, 2000). Mainframes provided a centralized place for data processing, owned by the organization but not by the users themselves (Otey, 2011).

Into the 1960s, the US government and researchers with the Advanced Research Projects Agency (ARPA) had a small number of large but geographically separated computing centers (Kleinrock, 2010). They called on J. C. R. Licklider from BBN Technologies (formerly Bolt, Beranek and Newman) to create a network of these computers to share information. Licklider referred to his ideas for this project in a 1963 memo as the "Intergalactic Computer Network" (Licklider, 1963). Licklider's idea would become ARPANET and evolve into the modern Internet. While not the cloud as we know it today, it had all the essential features we expect in the cloud in terms of accessing and sharing data, software, and hardware.

The emergence of personal computers in the 1970s and home computers in the 1980s moved computational power away from mainframes and to personal computers accessible to many more people. The current growth of cloud computing represents an attempt to restore many of the computing advantages originally provided by mainframes, but with the added advantages of Internet connected, geographically distributed, and scalable data storage and processing.

The two main theories to the origin of the term "cloud computing" both explain it as a marketing term. George Favaloro and Sean O'Sullivan from Compaq and NetCentric may have conceived of the idea in 1996 as part of an investment/marketing plan to provide hardware and software to Internet service providers (ISP). The second and more well-known origin of the term cloud computing comes from discussion at a Search Engine Strategy Conference in 2006 with Google's Chairman and CEO Eric Schmidt (Regalado, 2011). A few weeks later, Amazon unveils their beta version of Amazon Elastic Compute Cloud (EC2) (Amazon, 2006). Regardless of the origin of the term, the recognition of the needs satisfied by cloud computing existed for a long time. The suitability of the metaphor hints that the term may have had several instances of independent "discovery."

1.2 PRIVACY AND SECURITY CONCEPTS AND ISSUES

Privacy and security mean many things to different people. Here we identify and clarify our perspective on cloud data privacy and security.

Cloud data security has many facets:

- File content
- File metadata
- User identity
- Data availability

People usually think of cloud data storage security with respect to the files themselves. Who can read it? Who can change it? Who can delete it? The list of candidates includes you, those you give permission, your cloud storage provider, third-party data consumers, legal entities, and criminals. Those who can read your data can profit from it or hurt you with it. Those who can change it, possibly without your knowledge to deceive you. Those who can delete it can deny you access. Also, realize that deleting your data might make it unavailable only to you, but your cloud storage provider could keep it for their own business purposes. Furthermore, any of your data sold or given to third parties continues to exist.

Data remanence describes the issue of data or fragments of data remaining in physical memory after deletion. This occurs because deleting marks space with the file data as unused but does not overwrite the data. Computer forensic tools can read this unused space. This creates two problems for you when you delete your cloud storage data. First, it still exists on hardware owned by others and probably in multiple places all over the world. Second, physical memory used by you gets re-allocated to other customers. If the cloud provider does not properly erase this physical memory, hackers can run their own cyber-forensic tools to search the space given to them for valuable data. Encryption will not protect you if decryption occurs on these servers, since both cached instances of your files and the decryption key will exist in this memory (Bloomberg, 2011).

Cloud storage providers can effectively eliminate security issues related to data remanence by properly de-provisioning virtual machines as part of their policy. However, one must still verify with the cloud storage provider that they do address the data remanence issue using industry best practices.

Virtualized cloud storage has a number of security risks. Among these security risks include old virtualization images without the latest security fixes, corrupt images, and vulnerabilities in the virtualization manager. These security risks might allow malware on one VM to observe network traffic, attack other VMs or the VM manager itself.

Many cloud providers have begun promoting multi-tenancy instead of virtualization (Linthicum, 2010). Multi-tenant architectures allow different clients to share the same application without sharing the same data. This allows for greater scaling on the part of the cloud provider and more savings to the consumer. However, multi-tenant software can have security flaws that give hackers access to data of other users.

Some cloud storage providers have terms and conditions that give them unlimited use of data stored with them. This often means pictures and video, but could also mean creative thoughts, either copyrightable or patentable.

The "right to be forgotten" originated in the European Union (EU), but has gotten legal support in the United States and Argentina, among others. Now considered a human right, the right to be forgotten allows individuals to have publicly available online information about themselves permanently deleted. Laws to enforce the right to be forgotten can help individuals and companies recover from private and sensitive data disclosures. The right to be forgotten includes personal data reported by the press, which falls outside the scope of this book.

Not only do you need to protect the files themselves, you must also secure information about the files too. Cloud storage providers will collect metadata about your usage patterns, including network IP address, time, file size, file name, file action (add, modify, delete, etc.). Usage patterns correlated with other observed activities. Patterns showing your organization using certain software or access certain data before or after some observable action allows others to predict and anticipate your behavior and infer your motivations.

Consider the case where an observer has access to only your cell phone metadata for calls and text. This metadata includes who you call, when you call, from where you call, and how quickly you answer. From this limited metadata, researchers found they could predict the Big Five Personality traits (neuroticism, extraversion, conscientiousness, agreeableness, and openness) of the user significantly better than random (MONTJOYE et al., 2013). With more metadata available to cloud providers, insiders, and other observers, one can easily see the possibility of correlating cloud data storage interaction with other events.

Cloud data security should also include a consideration of information that could uniquely identify a person. Cloud storage providers may collect a variety of user data, such as real name, email, phone, physical address, IP address, MAC address, physical location (from

GPS or IP geolocation), contacts, browser history, and cloud storage usage patterns. They can collect much of this data through both client applications and server-side interfaces.

Cloud storage providers will use your data and metadata to improve their quality of service (QoS) to you. This affords justification to them for searching your data and metadata for clues to provide advertising links that generate clicks and sales to their advertisers. They might also sell this data to third parties. However, usage patterns could leak information about sensitive activities about individuals or companies. For example, a company might show more or less activity related to certain files before making public announcements. The ability to predict the timing and nature of such announcements could provide others with valuable insider information about the company.

Some providers may also scan your files for patterns of colors, shapes, or terms. In addition to looking for terms to use for targeted advertising or sale to third parties, cloud storage providers may scan images using face recognition software or other software to detect things like pornography or even commercial products appearing in you these images.

The HTTP protocol allows providers to track your browser history through the REFERER header field. This field gives the provider the site you visited just prior to their site and might also contain search query data. Accessing your cloud storage by logging in through a social media site might give the cloud storage provider permission to retrieve your social media data as well. Third-party cookies in your browser can also reveal to others at least the time patterns that you do things with your cloud storage. Smart phone applications that access cloud storage collect information about your location from Wi-Fi access points and about your contacts.

We include in our discussion of cloud data security the concept of data availability. People and organizations put data in the cloud because they want it available anywhere, anytime. Your inability to access your critical data represents a security concern, whether that unavailability comes from technical or legal issues, or malicious action. The legal and financial stability of the data storage provider deserves consideration. Bankruptcy or legal action against the company could make your data unavailable to you, temporarily or permanently, and with little notice for you to prepare alternatives. Also, such action could put your data in the hands of other entities and agencies. You should also consider your cloud storage provider's policies and procedures to protect their network from intrusions, denial of service attacks, malicious insiders, and hardware failures. The geographic location of the data center(s) can affect availability. Natural disasters far away can destroy your data or temporarily deny you access to it.

1.2.1 Your Data Versus Other People's Data

Data you put in cloud storage may belong to you or to others. Your data could contain private information about others too. This holds for individuals, companies, and academic institutions. This raises the issue of data ownership versus stewardship. Data stewardship seems most obvious when you deliberately collect information about others.

- Academic research surveys
- Business marketing surveys
- Customer resource management (CRM) data
- Employee payroll and billing
- Patient medical histories

Data you own includes sensitive information like tax or legal records, private email, and personal opinions. Remember that when you put your own personal opinions and other information in public clouds, they in some sense belong to others as well. You might keep your personal and professional lives separate, but not everyone understands or respects such compartmentalization. To many people, no separation exists between personal and professional attitudes. Your most gracious and respectful professional demeanor will not protect you from an offensive statement made in a personal context in a public cloud.

Data you think you own may contain sensitive information about others and therefore have stewardship issues. Consider these instances where your data also contains information about others:

- Mentions of other people
- Photos containing other people
- Contacts, phone numbers, addresses
- Email CC versus BCC

You have to think about the information you know about others and whether that information belongs to you or to them. Freedom of speech in the United States gives broad liberties to the kinds of information people make public. However, just because you can does not mean you should. The Golden Rule applies here, except we still have to deal with masochists.

The greatest threat to your privacy and security comes not from hackers (criminal or government), but from your family, friends, coworkers, and employees. You also represent the greatest privacy and security threat to them. Loose lips sink ships as they say. Before posting data to social media or sharing it with others, think about who it provides information about.

Consider the following two hypothetical (!) posts to social media:

- I skipped work to go drinking.
- Me and @johnsmith12345 skipped work to go drinking.

The first represents your data because it relates to you. The second contains other people's data. You might not get fired from your job for this, but your (former!) friend might.

Photos posted to Facebook of yourself that also include other people contain their data too. You might not consider the content of this image private or worry about security implications. However, other people in the photo may have their privacy and security jeopardized. People can find these photos through image searches of photo tags and through face-recognition data-mining.

You can jeopardize a person's privacy and security by making comments about their daily activity patterns, information about their children, or when they go on vacation. Criminals can assemble seemingly innocuous details about a person to build a profile they can use to their advantage.

The website http://pleaserobme.com/ uses locations from Twitter accounts to geolocate people, specifically those away from home. Recently, Britons received a warning that insurance companies might not pay claims on home burglaries if they find evidence online that the homeowner posted information about their absence from home (Perring, 2015).

Critical comments on social media about employers, co-workers, or students in the case of teachers have gotten people fired. Also, these comments might reveal information others consider private. Employers, especially school districts, can terminate employment for personal conduct not directly related to their job, for example, photos showing a person drinking alcohol or expressing controversial opinions, even in jest. Often, employers will even want access to their employees social media.

Your contact list may leak information about the social networks of other people. People in your contact list may not know one another, but it represents a link. If someone participates in extremist blog postings and has you on their contact list, then you become linked to that activity too. If people connect you to crazy/dangerous, then they will put you in that category too, and you may never fully convince them otherwise.

Emailing large numbers of people using CC instead of BCC exposes everyone's email address to everyone else. Spammers and hackers put high value on valid email addresses. If anyone who received one of these emails has their email account hacked, then everyone on the list becomes vulnerable to spammers and hackers. In addition, it reveals social network linkages. Inviting people to join groups by providing an email address, or emailing news story links to people gives others information about those people without their permission.

Sharing files with others via Dropbox or Google Drive can also jeopardize the security of your data and that of others. Default sharing options on these sites often allow those you share files with, to share those files with others. Etiquette says that invited guests should not themselves invite guests. The same should hold for sharing cloud data. Take care that default security settings on cloud data you choose to share does not allow others to share that data too. Also, realize this only prevents unintentional, one-click sharing and not intentional sharing.

You have a responsibility when accessing cloud data that belongs to you and to others. Retrieving data from the cloud on an unsecured or unapproved device can create problems for you and others. For example, many people read personal email or file attachments at work, for example photos. This constitutes a breach of privacy and security because these data get cached and decrypted on the company computer. If your company has an IT department, then you must be aware that they will routinely search computers for abuses of company resources. They will find the data you downloaded, which could lead to embarrassment or harm to you and others. Similar issues exist when employees by accident or malice download data from cloud storage to unauthorized devices.

You might put research data (academic or marketing) in the cloud to share with others for collaboration. While this data might not contain personally identifiable information about the people used in your research, the data records could contain enough unique values that someone could re-identify, with high probability, the people in the study by linking these records with similar records from other data sources. The US Census uses a number of strategies to prevent unauthorized disclosure of personally identifiable information.

1.2.2 Getting Your Data In and Out of the Cloud

People migrate their data to the cloud so they can access it anytime and anywhere. However, if you can get your data in and out of the cloud anytime and anywhere, then so can others.

Security issues arise at the endpoints and network connection. The device you use to access the cloud has security vulnerabilities. The cloud storage provider has vulnerabilities, both external and internal. Data in motion through the network also experiences security vulnerabilities.

Your device (phone, tablet, PC, XBox, etc.) and the software on it used to access cloud data creates privacy and security risks. The device itself may auto-connect to a common wireless network service set identifier (SSID). A hacker can set up a fake Wi-Fi hotspot with that same SSID and your device will happily connect to it. This makes it possible for man-in-the-middle attacks that give attackers full access to your security credentials and data. Old versions of the operating system or software with security holes may give attackers a base to target your data. Software, including web browsers, used to access your data may remember passwords or keep you logged in to those accounts. The devices may store a local copy of your data. Thieves can easily steal small devices like smart phones and tablets. Others may borrow your phone too. Both situations leave your data vulnerable to theft or discovery.

Wi-Fi hotspots, including your home Wi-Fi, may expose your data to others. Hackers can set up evil-twin Wi-Fi access points to mimic legitimate Wi-Fi networks. Connecting to an evil-twin allows hackers to sniff your unencrypted traffic or redirect you to fake sites to get your login credentials.

Using HTTPS/SSL/TLS to connect to the Internet and to your cloud storage provider does not guarantee privacy or the security of your data. Companies or hackers can set up proxy appliances to intercept network traffic, thereby inserting themselves as the man-in-the-middle of your secure network connections. With a proxy appliance present on the network, your browser or application securely connects to the proxy, which can decrypt, inspect, and modify your data, before sending it on its own secure connection to your cloud provider. Note that some antivirus software also does HTTPS/SSL/TLS inspection.

You can usually detect a proxy appliance when the website that you connect to uses an Extended Validation (EV) certificate. HTTPS-capable web servers provide a certificate signed by a Certificate Authority (CA) to prove its identity as part of the connection setup. Servers using Extended Validation (EV) certificates enable browsers like Firefox and Chrome to verify a direct secure connection via their own list of trusted CA. Figures 1.1 and 1.2 below show how a secure connection to Dropbox should appear in Chrome and Firefox.

If you do not see the green padlock then you do not have a secure connection and may have a proxy appliance between you and the Internet. Forewarned means forearmed.

Figure 1.1 Extended Validation (EV) certificate in Chrome.

Figure 1.2 Extended Validation (EV) certificate in Firefox.

Finally, your cloud storage provider completes the chain of data privacy and security vulnerabilities, which can exist in network hardware, computer servers, the physical facility, staff, and policy. Cloud providers use virtualization or multi-tenancy to efficiently manage their resources. Hackers can exploit software bugs or use forensic tools to access this data. Vulnerabilities exist to the physical security of the data centers from outside security threats such as man-made and natural disasters. Company policies regarding who has access to customer data and under what circumstances also has an affect on data security, as well as the thoroughness of the employee vetting process.

1.2.3 Legal Versus Criminal Threats

In this section we highlight the scope of legal and criminal threats to data placed in cloud storage.

1.2.3.1 Legal Threats

Legal threats to your cloud storage data will typically come from the following:

- Cloud provider terms of use
- Copyright and file-sharing
- Civil litigation
- Legal search warrants
- Local laws given your location
- Local laws given your cloud storage data center

Cloud data storage providers may have terms of use which may permit them broad access to your metadata and to your data content. Terms of use may have ambiguous language that makes confidentiality ambiguous. Legal ambiguity could mean going to court to defend your privacy and data security, a long and costly process with no guarantee of success. Remember, you agreed to the terms and conditions, ambiguities included, in exchange for free cloud data storage. Fee-based accounts should give you more privacy and security, but do not assume this.

The Recording Industry Association of America (RIAA) and the Motion Picture Association of America (MPAA), among others, have concerns about cloud storage used to illegally share copyrighted material. The Digital Millennium Copyright Act (DMCA) gives copyright holders legal authority to act against suspected copyright violators. While DMCA tactics and enforcement remains controversial, these organizations do have a valid point. They sell copyrighted material for use by one person. If that person makes copies and gives or sells them to others, then they have potentially deprived the copyright holder of material benefit. This issue does not happen for physical items like cars. When you purchase a car, you can use it or let some else use it. You cannot make free copies of the car and give them away. However, you can do this with digital media and this creates difficulties for copyright holders.

Civil litigation, such as from business lawsuits or divorce, may give others legal access to your cloud data. Requests for this data will go to your cloud provider, who will likely comply with any legitimate legal request. As a result, unknown others may view your sensitive data and download and archived by the court to places not under your control and for an unknown time. Furthermore, the data they view or download may not in fact relate to the litigation, but get included because of the scope of the data request.

Legal warrants could make a significant amount of your data accessible to law enforcement and whatever agency (public or private) tasked to analyze your data. This means others will have full access to your data, with no guarantee of what will happen to this data or how it will get used or by whom.

Police stops and security checkpoints give law enforcement a warrant or justification to access your data. The legal status of devices in the United States remains dynamic and ambiguous. This means both you and authorities could misinterpret your responsibilities. In the United States, a password might fall under the Fifth Amendment, but a biometric lock might not. As a case in point, a court in Virginia recently ruled that a password has Fifth Amendment protection because it represents knowledge, while a fingerprint does not because it serves as a physical key (BODI, 2015). This means those who protect their devices and data with biometric security lose their Fifth Amendment rights. These people still have their Fourth Amendment right to illegal search and seizure, so law enforcement must still obtain a warrant. However, this still does not provide adequate safeguards to data privacy. A police officer in California had to resign and face charges for unauthorized access to a computer and illegally copying data for sending nude photos of women from their cell phones to his while in police custody (Serna, 2014).

Given the current legal ambiguities over cloud data and electronic media in general, authorities might consider action to protecting your data after they confront you as unlawful. Your refusal to allow authorities access to your device and the data accessible from it could result in your arrest. Even if you acted correctly, you could suffer from a misinterpretation of data privacy and security laws. In such situations, even if you win the legal case, you still lose in terms of time, money, stress, and opportunities lost by dealing with the situation.

Local laws governing both your physical location and the physical location of your data affect the security of that data. You might have data secured in cloud storage physically located in the United States. However, travel outside the United States could put you in a situation where law enforcement in other countries can compel you to show them this data through your device. Alternatively, cloud storage data centers outside the United States have different laws governing who can access your data and under what circumstances.

1.2.3.2 Criminal Threats
The list below shows categories of motives for attacking your data and cloud storage.

- *Exploit*. Data of value to you may have value to others.
- *Deny*. Temporarily preventing you from getting your data may benefit someone else.
- *Destroy*. Permanently destroying your data might benefit someone else.
- *Deceive*. Subtle changes to your data that may go unnoticed until they cause a problem.
- *Usurp*. Others use your storage for their own purposes, possibly hiding illegal content.

Your personal data has value to others for many reasons. Cyber-stalkers want your data to establish some personal or intimate relationship with you. Cyber-bullies want to harass or embarrass you. Note that the data about you they reveal could damage your reputation such that it results in loss of your job or valuable opportunities. Criminals can use this information to coerce action or extort money from you. Your data may help criminals steal your identity, perhaps by helping them guess answers to security questions for various online accounts.

Businesses experience many of the same threats as individuals. In addition, industrial espionage could occur where criminals obtain information about your business strategy, contracts, customer relations management (CRM) data, or other intellectual property and use or sell it. Metadata about your company could leak information that gives criminals insider information to help them with business negotiations or investing.

The term "doxing" refers to the publishing of personal or sensitive data about people or organizations for the purpose of vigilante justice, harassment, embarrassment, extortion, or coercion. Organizations like Anonymous, AntiSec, and LulzSec use doxing to draw attention to perceived injustices. Most people and organizations do not have to worry about these groups. However, conflicts occur between people, friends, coworkers, employees; and you might provoke a person who will do something like this.

Celebrities represent obvious targets for hackers seeking sensitive cloud data. Recently, a number of celebrities had nude photos of themselves downloaded from their private Apple iCloud accounts in an event called "The Fappening." Hackers used brute force attacks on names, passwords, and security questions to obtain the data. Apple denied a breach in their security and instead blamed weak passwords and lack of two-factor encryption (Berlind, 2014).

Violently radical organizations use the Internet to intimidate their enemies. They use the Internet to spread information and they use it to find information to use against those who oppose them. A white supremacist group targeted a federal judge for assassination by circulating her address and family photos on the Internet. Two years later, the judge came home to find her husband and mother murdered execution-style. In this case, the killer did not have connections to white supremacy, but the implications seem clear (Southern Poverty Law Center, 2005). More sensitive information exists in the cloud now than it did in 2005. The more strangers and enemies know about you or your company, the more damage they can do to you and the people and things you care about.

1.3 CLOUD STORAGE

1.3.1 What Is It?

The cloud storage data model specifies how digital data gets stored and retrieved across multiple servers in possibly geographically different locations and managed by a hosting provider. Cloud storage uses a logical memory model that allows providers to store your data on multiple servers in different locations in a way transparent to you.

At a minimum, cloud storage includes space for some amount of data and a simple interface to manage files in the storage. Often this involves creating a special folder on your computer and monitoring file activity in it. Dropbox belongs to this category of cloud storage. More elaborate cloud storage includes sophisticated SaaS that seamlessly integrates with backend cloud storage. Google Docs offers this kind of service for Google Drive.

This book focuses on security concerns for users of cloud data storage and those using SaaS. We do not address the additional security issues related to those needing PaaS and IaaS. Thus, this book provides information and guidance for cloud data storage users who do not have significant control of security of the software or cloud infrastructure.

1.3.2 Case Studies: Comparison of Cloud Storage Security

We now compare security features for a number of cloud storage providers. Table 1.1 does not provide a complete list or an endorsement. Instead, we want to indicate the range and availability of some important security features.

The cloud storage providers we compare all have some amount of free (non-trial) storage, and we compare their security on these plans. Note that in some cases, paid plans will have additional security options.

We compare security based on the criteria of two-factor authentication, Extended Validation (EV) certificates, encryption strength, zero-knowledge encryption, regulatory compliance, and location of data centers. We do not delve in to the details of how individual providers maintain security in their data centers.

Two-step or two-factor authentication requires the user to enter two pieces of information to login, a password and a one-time passcode sent to the user by text, email, or retrieved by the user with an app. As a variation on this method, the Google Authenticator App has users store a shared secret from the website on their device. To log in to the site, users must provide their username, password, and a one-time password generated by the app.

Table 1.1 Selected Security and Privacy Features of Free Cloud Storage Providers						
Provider	Two factor	EV for HTTPS	Encryption	Zero Knowledge	Compliance	Data Centers
Amazon Cloud Drive https://www. amazon.com/ clouddrive	no	no	no	no	Safe Harbor	
Box https://www. box.com/	yes	no	AES-256	no	Safe Harbor, APEC	
Copy https://www. copy.com/	no	no	AES-256	no		
Dropbox https:// www.dropbox.com/	yes	yes	AES-256	no	Safe Harbor	
Google Drive http://www.google. com/drive/	yes	useless	no	no	Safe Harbor	
iCloud https:// www.icloud.com/	yes	yes	AES-128 min	no		
OneDrive https:// onedrive.live.com/	yes	yes	no	no		
Mega https://mega. co.nz/	no	no	AES-128	yes	Safe Harbor	EU, NZ
SpiderOak https:// spideroak.com/	yes	no	AES-256	yes[a,b]	Safe Harbor, HIPAA capable	
Tresorit https:// tresorit.com/	yes	yes	AES-256	yes	Safe Harbor	EU
Wuala https://www. wuala.com/	no	no	AES-256	yes[a]	Swiss DPA/DPO	Switzerland, Germany, France

[a]Shared files get decrypted on their servers.
[b]Zero-knowledge encryption via client application.

In addition to the above two-factor authentication strategies, Google will optionally remember your computer and use it as the passcode. Google Chrome also supports USB security keys for two-step verification. Once you register this key with your Google account, it unlocks your account similarly to a house key that unlocks your house, after you provide your username and password.

Extended Validation (EV) certificates provide an extra level of security that verifies you have no one intercepting your data while in motion between you and your cloud storage. Note that Google probably does use EV certificates, but their infrastructure prevents browsers from providing confirmation to users that they have a secure connection with Google. This makes Google EV useless for privacy and security from the user's perspective with respect to independent confirmation from a CA.

Encryption strength describes the algorithm used to encrypt your data. NIST recommends AES-256. Server-side encryption may use convergent encryption. This approach uses a cryptographic hash of the unencrypted file as the encryption key. The hash itself gets encrypted with the user password. This results in the same file always having the same encrypted form. Cloud storage providers use this technique for data de-duplication because the same file only gets stored once. However, it means a third party can check if you have a file by following the same procedure on their own file. If their encrypted file matches yours, then they know you have the file.

Zero-knowledge encryption means the cloud storage provider does not have the ability to decrypt your data. Data encryption occurs on the client, then gets sent via a secure connection to the provider. This protects your data in transit and at the provider's data centers. Since only you have the decryption key, your data cannot get decrypted without your knowledge (unless someone guesses or steals from you your decryption key!). Zero-knowledge encryption protects cloud storage providers too, because they have no way to know the content of the files they store and this makes them less vulnerable to legal issues.

However, zero-knowledge encryption does not always apply to shared data. Some cloud storage providers who advertise zero-knowledge encryption break this promise for file sharing. To share your files, these providers might get your decryption key and decrypt your file on their servers and distribute it in cleartext to those who you shared it with. Finally, providers may only offer zero-knowledge encryption when using their client application and not when using a browser interface.

Participation in regulatory compliance provides evidence for a commitment to privacy and data security. Many standards exist for data privacy and security. Here we consider only the ones most commonly offered in free cloud storage accounts.

Safe Harbor compliance indicates that the cloud storage provider meets the data privacy and security requirements of the EU Data

Protection Directive. The Swiss Data Protection Act (DPA) and Data Protection Ordinance (DPO) have more strict data privacy and security requirements. The Asia-Pacific Economic Cooperation (APEC) has its own standards for data exchanged between its member countries. The Health Insurance Portability and Accountability Act (HIPAA) specifies how cloud storage providers should secure personal health data. Note that many cloud storage providers do offer guarantees of regulatory compliance in paid plans.

We include data center locations in our security comparison because laws regarding privacy and security can vary significantly from country to country. Storing your data in the cloud in your country could put your data under the jurisdiction of another country. We prefer that cloud storage providers give their customers a readily accessible and exhaustive list of the countries with their data centers. You cannot assume that a provider based in your country has data centers only in your country. Often they will lease space with global data centers, so your data could physically reside anywhere in the world. Data privacy and security protections you expect in your country might not apply in countries where your provider stores it.

We looked to the cloud storage provider websites for security information for our evaluation. Our failure to identify privacy and security features does not mean they do not exist. However, we suggest caution when considering cloud storage from providers who do not clearly and obviously state useful details about how they protect your privacy and data security.

1.4 CLOUD-BASED DATA SHARING

We distinguish between cloud storage and cloud data sharing because sharing data with others adds additional security issues to those of storing data for personal use only. Cloud-based data sharing includes social media, shared file storage, and collaborative work spaces. Individuals use cloud-based data sharing to exchange photos, music, or thoughts with a small group of friends. Companies use cloud-based data sharing to enable employees to access data remotely and to collaborate with customers. Research institutions want to collect, analyze, and share data with others. This has tremendous value for science.

Issues to consider for cloud-based data sharing fall into three categories:

* Member trust
* Access control
* Sharing mechanism

Member trust represents the greatest security consideration for cloud-based data sharing. Here you must trust all those with access to act responsibly. Once you give people access to your data, you make yourself vulnerable to their mistakes or malice. You have to trust those you share data with to (1) not share data with non-group members, (2) not download data to unsecured devices or on unsecured networks, and (3) not upload inappropriate or illegal content.

Access control means the mechanism for you to allow and revoke access to your shared cloud data. Revoking permission of a member might mean changing the password for everyone, then communicating that change to them through some alternate secure channel. Revoking access to some files could mean having to re-encrypt those files with a new password and exchanging that new password with remaining group members. More sophisticated access control using public key infrastructure (PKI) allows for adding and removing member public keys for authentication and authorization.

The file sharing mechanisms implemented by cloud storage providers have their own security issues to consider. Secret URLs enable the sharing of cloud data with people who do not have accounts with the cloud storage provider. These secret URLs contain the credentials needed to retrieve your data. Security issues arise because browsers will save these URLs in their histories, people can send them to non-authorized people, the email containing the URL might get compromised, and the habit of URL shortening sends this secret URL to a shortening service that maps it to a shorter URL. Shorter URLs make it easier for brute-force attacks to find secret shared data links.

Zero-knowledge encryption may not apply to shared cloud data. Cloud storage providers may need to obtain your encryption key to decrypt your shared file on their server before sending it to others.

1.5 SUMMARY

The software, platforms, and infrastructures that we call the "Cloud" have existed in some sense since the late 1960s. Cloud data storage privacy and security issues affect the data itself, metadata about you and your data, and the movement of the data between your device and the cloud storage hardware. You may put data owned by others in to cloud storage for work or research. Even if you consider the data your own, it could contain sensitive information about others. A variety of legal threats to your data privacy and security exist, including cloud provider terms of use, legal warrants, and different laws across geographic jurisdictions. Criminals may want your data for many other reasons than just identity theft. Sharing data in the cloud brings additional privacy and security concerns, including trust among participants and managing access control.

REFERENCES

Amazon, 2006. Announcing Amazon Elastic Compute Cloud (Amazon EC2) – beta. [Online] 24 August. https://aws.amazon.com/about-aws/whats-new/2006/08/24/announcing-amazon-elastic-compute-cloud-amazon-ec2---beta/ (accessed April 2015).

Amrehn, E., Elliott, J., 2012. 45 (40)Years of Mainframe Virtualization: CP-67/CMS and VM/370 to z/VM. IBM Corporation. [Online] Available from: https://www-950.ibm.com/events/wwe/grp/grp019.nsf/vLookupPDFs/7%20-%20VM-45-JahreHistory-EA-J-Elliott%20%5BKompatibilit%C3%A4tsmodus%5D/$file/7%20-%20VM-45-JahreHistory-EA-J-Elliott%20%5BKompatibilit%C3%A4tsmodus%5D.pdf (accessed 30.11.14).

Bergin, T.J., 2000. 50 Years of Army Computing: From ENIAC to MSRC. Army Research Lab, Aberdeen Proving Ground, MD. [Online] Available from: http://www.arl.army.mil/www/pages/shared/documents/50_years_of_army_computing.pdf (accessed 30.11.14).

Berlind, D., 2014. The Naked Truth About Internet Security. The Programmable Web. [Online] 17 September. http://www.programmableweb.com/news/naked-truth-about-internet-security/analysis/2014/09/17 (accessed April 2015).

Bloomberg, J., 2011. Data Remanence: Cloud Computing Shell Game. [Online]. Available from: http://cloudcomputing.sys-con.com/node/1841820 (accessed 30.11.14).

Bodi, A.E., 2015. Phones, fingerprints, and the Fifth Amendment. Am. Crim. Law Rev. [Online] 21 January. http://www.americancriminallawreview.com/aclr-online/phones-fingerprints-and-fifth-amendment/ (accessed April 2015).

Kleinrock, L., 2010. Personal History/Biography: the Birth of the Internet. [Online] Available from: http://www.lk.cs.ucla.edu/personal_history.html (accessed 30.11.14).

Licklider, J.C.R., 1963. Topics for Discussion at the Forthcoming Meeting, Memorandum For: Members and Affiliates of the Intergalactic Computer Network. Advanced Research Projects Agency. [Online] Available from: http://www.kurzweilai.net/memorandum-for-members-and-affiliates-of-the-intergalactic-computer-network (accessed 30.11.14).

Linthicum, D., 2010. The silly debate over multitenancy. InfoWorld [Online] 9 April. Available from: http://www.infoworld.com/article/2683529/cloud-computing/the-silly-debate-over-multitenancy.html (accessed 30.11.14).

Mell, P., Grance, T., 2011. The NIST Definition of Cloud Computing. National Institute of Standards and Technology Special Publication 800-145. [Online] Available from: http://csrc.nist. gov/publications/nistpubs/800-145/SP800-145.pdf (accessed 30.11.14).

Montjoye, Y.-A., Quoidbach, J., Robic, F., Pentland, A., 2013. Predicting people personality using novel mobile phone-based metrics. Social Computing, Behavioral-Cultural Modeling and Prediction. Lecture Notes in Computer Science. [Online] Volume 7812, pp. 48−55. http://reality-commons.media.mit.edu/download.php?file=deMontjoye2013predicting-citation.pdf   (accessed April 2015).

Nedbal, D., Stieninger, M., 2014. Exploring the economic value of a cloud computing solution and its contribution to green IT. Int. J. Bus. Process Integration Manag. 7 (1), 62−72.

Otey, M., 2011. Is the Cloud Really Just the Return of Mainframe Computing? SQL Server Pro. [Online] 22 March. Available from: http://sqlmag.com/cloud/cloud-really-just-return-mainframe-computing (accessed 30.11.14).

Perring, R., 2015. No 'hot-dog legs' - Keep holiday selfies OFF Facebook or have insurance claims REJECTED. Sunday Express [Online] 23 April. http://www.express.co.uk/news/uk/572365/Holiday-insurance-claims-rejected-selfies-Facebook (accessed April 2015).

Regalado, A., 2011. Who coined 'cloud computing'?. MIT Technical Review. [Online] 31 October. http://www.technologyreview.com/news/425970/who-coined-cloud-computing/ (accessed 30.11.14).

Serna, G., 2014. Ex-CHP officer charged with two felonies in nude-photo sharing case. Los Angeles Times [Online] 3 November. http://www.latimes.com/local/lanow/la-me-ln-chp-officer-photo-trading-20141031-story.html (accessed April 2015).

Southern Poverty Law Center, 2005. Family of judge targeted by hate group murdered. Southern Poverty Law Center. [Online] 1 March. http://www.splcenter.org/get-informed/news/family-of-judge-targeted-by-hate-group-murdered (accessed April 2015).

CHAPTER 2

Application Data in the Cloud

The future of computing will no doubt be intertwined with cloud storage. Already, vendors of applications are moving not only their applications (office suites, backup services, email) into the cloud as services, but rely on the cloud for "secure" storage of user-created content. These applications are perhaps the most obvious examples of the cloud being used to store and process information, some of which may be considered sensitive or at least private to the user.

There is also a trend for moving what is commonly referred to as social media to the cloud as well. In fact, the cloud is a key component of all social media. It provides a common place to store information that can be shared with friends, groups, and the world. The social media cloud-based service is either delivered through a web browser or as an application (app) downloaded from the cloud and installed on a device, such as a smartphone or tablet. The majority of the content is stored in the cloud.

From a security a standpoint, there is plenty of opportunity for mischief. First, if the app is downloaded from an app site such as Apple's App Store or Google's Marketplace, the user must trust that what is being downloaded performs as advertised: nothing more, nothing less. The user must also trust that the app has not been modified to perform unwanted actions, contains no backdoors, and has been coded without any flaws that can be exploited and result in a security compromise. Assuming the first two caveats are screened for by the App Store/Marketplace, the third one, "coding flaws that result in a security compromise" is the unknown-unknown that lurks in every piece of code.

That may seem like an outrageous or paranoid statement, but a visit to the United States Computer Emergency Readiness Team (US-CERT) website will put the concept of code vulnerability into perspective:

> The US-CERT Cyber Security Bulletin provides a summary of new vulnerabilities that have been recorded by the National Institute of Standards and Technology

(NIST) National Vulnerability Database (NVD) in the past week. The NVD is sponsored by the Department of Homeland Security (DHS) National Cybersecurity and Communications Integration Center (NCCIC) / United States Computer Emergency Readiness Team (US-CERT). For modified or updated entries, please visit the NVD, which contains historical vulnerability information.
(US-CERT, 2015)

What you will find there is a list of the security flaws discovered this past week for applications that are in use by end users, commercial websites, government websites — places you visit and applications and operating systems that you use.

While application security is not the main focus of this book, the security of the data created and stored by these applications is. One of the takeaways of this chapter is that *if* the applications can be compromised, so can your data. The key point, however, is that if you trust your private information to the cloud via service providers, who will have access to that information and what will they use it for?

Throughout this chapter we will use a case study methodology to present and analyze various security issues that arise when using the cloud to store information. The case study will follow this basic outline and organization:

1. Begin by asking questions that help focus the security and information privacy analysis associated with each application type.
2. Define the key security concepts and background information to assist the reader in understanding the analysis.
3. Provide a narrative to explain the research methods and results along with questions and problems that were discovered during the analysis.
4. Conclusion that addresses the security question(s).

In the following sections, using this case study outline, we will investigate the security of cloud-based email, cloud backup services, social media, and cloud-based password managers.

2.1 APPLICATIONS

2.1.1 Email

Email, or electronic mail, is a system that allows the exchange of information between one or more users. Email can be used to send text, images, documents, and files of all types to one or more recipients.

2.1.2 Background

Email, one of the original forms of social media, is even older than the web and contains a detailed description of our personal and professional history. The concept of email has been around since the 1960s, where implementations were created and used by a number of university research labs, most notably MIT. This was pre-Internet and operated through dialup lines into an IBM mainframe computing system. The Advanced Research Project Agency (ARPA) took email to the next level with the advent of what is now called the internet. ARPAnet was a digital communication system that connected universities and government research facilities together for the purpose of experimenting and exchanging research information. This provided the test bed for the concepts and protocols for what is now known as the public internet.

Email is based on a client—server architecture where email is sent from many clients (users) to a server, which routes the email message to the intended destination where it is stored on a mail server and read by the recipient.

There are two server types involved in sending email: the Simple Mail Transfer Protocol (SMTP) server, which receives email from the user's client and routes it to the destination where it is stored on the recipient's *mail server*.

In the simplest case, the mail server can be a single computer running an SMTP and mail server service, which is connected to the internet. Email is provided globally through millions of instances of this configuration as businesses and email providers implemented and maintained their individual email systems. As the use of email has increased and internet access became commonplace, that model has given way to large cloud-base mail systems that support millions of users worldwide. Email systems, such as Gmail, Yahoo! Mail, and Outlook.com (formerly Hotmail), provide free cloud-based email to consumers using common web browser technology. Similar web-based email is provided to businesses and individuals who purchase and register domains through service providers, such as GoDaddy and 1and1.

There are four major areas of vulnerability in email:

1. The sender's and receiver's device (desktop, laptop, phone, tablet)
2. The email client application (web browser, Outlook, Thunderbird, Mail, Mailbox, etc.)

3. Email in transit from client to client (data-in-motion)
4. Storage on the mail server (data-at-rest)
5. End user behavior

These five areas of vulnerability are vital components of the overall security posture that could provide vectors for attackers to infiltrate email cloud storage and thereby bypass existing cloud security mechanisms. As an example:

1. Device security – If a user's device is compromised, it is possible to obtain the username and password that are associated with the email account. That would provide direct and authenticated access to email that is stored in the cloud.
2. Email client – It is also possible that there are security flaws in the email client that can be exploited, or there are flaws in other applications that are running on the device that have vulnerabilities that can be used to access email account information. Applications, including mobile device apps, have been developed that contain backdoors, data harvesting and exfiltration capabilities that users willingly install as free apps on their devices. It is important to read the fine print in the terms of service (TOS) and privacy policy.
3. In transit communication – It is also possible to intercept email data while in transit between the client sending the email and being received at the email server. Until recently, most email was sent in cleartext and could be easily intercepted and read with little effort. Currently most browser-based email is sent using encryption provided as part of the Hypertext Transfer Protocol Secure (HTTPS), which layers HTTP on top of the SSL/TLS security protocol to provide secure transport between client and server.
4. End user behavior – End users can be targeted by attackers using a variety of mechanisms, such as phishing, where the user plays an active role by clicking on an email attachment or on a web link from someone they know. This technique can be used to compromise the user's security, the security of others on the network, and data stored on local servers and in the cloud. A recent example was publicized where an email was sent to a user in the United States State Department, which resulted in compromising the State Department's network. This compromise was then used to infiltrate the unclassified network of the White House where data, including the daily schedule for the president of the United States, was stored.

This type of vulnerability has been around for years and is still effective because it exploits a well-known dynamic vulnerability: human behavior. The solution is user training and user awareness.

The focus of this section is to identify the security issues involved in using cloud-based email and to investigate how these issues are addressed by a cross section of currently available cloud-based implementations. Given the four areas identified above, our emphasis is on number four, which involves the storage of email and attachments.

2.1.3 Case Studies: Comparison of Cloud-Based Email Security (Gmail, Outlook.com (Hotmail), Yahoo! Mail)

2.1.3.1 Questions
How secure is cloud-based email? Can email and attachments be read by anyone other than the sender and receiver? Is privacy at risk? What can be done to make email more secure?

2.1.3.2 Security Concepts
As mentioned before, there are two areas of concern from a security perspective when sending and receiving email: the transmission of the email and the storage of the email. These are referred to as data in motion and data at rest, respectively. When data, email in this case, is sent from one user to another it passes through a number of routers and servers before it is finally delivered to its destination where it is stored. Using HTTPS can be used in browser-based email to encrypt email traffic between source and destination. If only HTTP is used, email is usually clear text or base-64 encoded, meaning that it is transferred from source to destination in a format that can be easily read, hence it is not secure. HTTP can be used to transfer encrypted email content, which is considered secure because it is encrypted during transmission.

After email arrives at its destination, text and attachments can be encrypted before it is stored. Encryption is a method of converting data, in this case an email message text, into an encoded form using a secret key and an algorithm that renders the data unreadable without knowledge of the secret key. When data is encrypted, there is a low probability that anyone other than the receiving party who has the secret key will be able to decrypt the data and convert it back into a readable form. (*Note*: "Low probability" does not mean zero. There are techniques that can be used to crack encrypted text if someone has enough motivation.)

2.1.3.3 Personally Identifiable Information (PII)

The term PII is defined in OMB Memorandum M-07-1616 refers to information that can be used to distinguish or trace an individual's identity, either alone or when combined with other personal or identifying information that is linked or linkable to a specific individual. The definition of PII is not anchored to any single category of information or technology. Rather, it requires a case-by-case assessment of the specific risk that an individual can be identified. In performing this assessment, it is important for an agency to recognize that non-PII can become PII whenever additional information is made publicly available — in any medium and from any source — that, when combined with other available information, could be used to identify an individual.

(GSA, 2015)

2.1.3.4 Methods and Results

To determine the level of security provided by cloud-based email providers, we examine the service providers TOS agreements, privacy policies, and other publically available information.

In this section we evaluate Gmail, Yahoo! Mail, and Outlook.com, formerly Hotmail. These email services are accessed (typically) through a web browser or a specialized mobile device app. These email services are cloud-based SAAS with email content stored in the cloud.

2.1.3.5 Data-in-Motion

All three email providers use HTTPS in the transmission of email between clients and servers. This provides a secure connection for data in motion. Here is an example of the URL for signing on to Gmail at gmail.com:

> https://accounts.google.com/ServiceLogin?service = mail&continue=
> https://mail.google.com/mail/

The HTTPS protocol is used for signing in to the service, which provides secure transmission of the username and password during authentication. HTTPS is also used during the email session. This is also true for Yahoo! Mail and Outlook.com.

Recently it was discovered that Google data, including Gmail, was being sent among Google data centers located throughout the world in an unencrypted form. Google moves data among their data centers to provide load balancing, data backup, faster access, etc. In reporting on

Edward Snowden, the *UK Guardian* revealed (2015) that this data was being intercepted by the National Security Agency while in transit between Google servers. While data in transit from a Gmail user to the Google email server was protected using encryption, data in motion was not secure between and among Google data centers. Google issued a press release indicating that they were fixing the problem and that in the future all data in motion would be encrypted. Yahoo! and Microsoft also issued similar statements indicating they are increasing their data-in-motion security.

2.1.3.6 Data at Rest

HTTPS provides data security and privacy between the user and the service provider's servers. But what happens after the email is delivered to the server? Is it secure during storage? Does anyone have access to the email content when it is stored in the cloud?

The short answer is that none of the providers encrypt email that is stored in the cloud. They do encrypt and protect login information, but not the actual contents of email.

2.1.3.7 Physical Security

It is also important that email providers protect the facilities where data is stored and control the physical access to the servers that store the email.

According to Yahoo!'s website, "Yahoo! maintains reasonable physical, electronic, and procedural safeguards that comply with federal regulations to protect personal information (PII) about you." From this statement we can assume that Yahoo! maintains secure physical structures and personnel access control over their cloud data and have procedures and policies that comply with federal regulation to protect PII. Federal regulations are described in detail in Chapter 4. Unfortunately, federal regulations do not require data at rest be encrypted. What this means from a security perspective is that if someone is able to breach the physical or procedural safeguards, they have access to your data.

2.1.3.8 Information Collected by Email Service Providers

Email systems contain a wealth of personal information. Most of these services provide online calendars, contact lists, schedules, chat sessions, as well as email communications. When signing up for these *free* services, users are required to provide certain information in exchange for the free service. While this information is volunteered by the user of the service, other information is combined and aggregated to provide a behavioral profile of the user. As an example of what information is gathered, aggregated, and used, can be found in the privacy policy and TOS agreements that users agree to when signing up for the service. You do read these carefully before you agree, right? As an example of what the email service provider "may" collect:

- Personal information that you *freely* provide when you register
  - Your name, email address, telephone number, birth date, gender, postal code, occupation, industry, and personal interests
  - For some financial products and services they might also ask for:
    - Your address, Social Security number, credit card number, and information about your assets
- Personal information the email service provider collects when you use their products or services, This includes:
  - Which services you use
  - Which pages you visit
  - How you use the services
  - How you interact with ads – which ads you click on
- Information about you obtained from other companies
- Information about your transactions
- Information about your use of financial products and services
- Device and browser information
  - IP address
  - Device identifiers – MAC address
  - Cookie information
  - Software and hardware attributes
  - Operating system and browser versions
- Information stored by the provider on their server logs
  - Search queries
  - Location information
  - Access dates and times
- Local storage – service providers may also store information they collect on your device

As a side note, collecting software and hardware attributes can be used to profile and uniquely identify a specific computer or device. This can be used to identify different online personas as actually being the same person. For example, suppose Alice creates an email account, bob@gmail.com and then signs up for a Facebook account using that email address, under the pseudo-name Charlie. Alice also uses the same device to check work email at acme.com. Using device profiling and access time analysis, Alice, Bob, and Charlie can be linked together, and with high probability it can be determined that they are the same person. Information gathered from these accounts and their associated cookies can be aggregated with data collected at signup to build a more robust demographic and behavioral profile of Alice.

2.1.3.9 From Google's Privacy Policy

> ...we may replace past names associated with your Google Account so that you are represented consistently across all our services. If other users already have your email, or other information that identifies you, we may show them your publicly visible Google Profile information, such as your name and photo.
>
> *(Google, 2015)*

It appears that there is a possibility that people who communicate with Bob on Facebook may be shown a profile and picture of Alice if Alice uses email and other services under her own name.

2.1.3.10 How Email Service Providers Use the Information

So, what happens to all of this information after it is collected? To begin with, Yahoo! is upfront with what they do with the information and your personal privacy:

> When you register with Yahoo! and sign in to our services, you are not anonymous to us.
>
> *(Yahoo!, 2015)*

Yahoo! and Google generally adhere to a similar core set of personal identifying information (PII) uses. They use this information to customize advertising and content, suggest/provide products and services, improve their services, conduct research, and provide anonymous reporting for internal and external clients.

They also provide the information to trusted partners under confidentiality agreements. These companies may use your personal information to communicate with you about offers from marketing partners. However, these companies do not have any independent right to share this information, according to the provider's privacy policy.

Personal information that is collected by these services is also subject to applicable state and federal laws. They are also subject to civil litigation. They must respond to subpoenas, court orders, legal process, and national security letters. A national security letter is effectively an administrative subpoena, issued by a federal agency, requiring the production of certain limited types of information held by third-party custodians (DOJ, 2015). What this means is that an administrative agency, such as the Federal Bureau of Investigation (FBI), can compel the disclosure of customer records from internet service providers, which includes email transactions, without a court order. A court order would be required if content is requested. In addition, the service provider can be prohibited from informing you that your data and information is the subject of a national security letter. You will not be notified.

Information can also be requested in civil litigation, such as divorce, medical malpractice, and breach of contract. This would require a subpoena.

In addition to legal investigation, email service provides can use all the data they collect for internal investigations when they suspect fraud, potential threats to persons, and violations of their terms of use.

2.1.3.11 Where Email Service Providers Differ

Beyond the legal issues of access to email which all service provides adhere to, our initial question still needs to be addressed: can anyone access/read my email and attachments other the sender, and the receiver(s)?

2.1.3.12 From Google's Terms of Service

Our automated systems analyze your content (including emails) to provide you personally relevant product features, such as customized search results, tailored advertising, and spam and malware detection. This analysis occurs as the content is sent, received, and when it is stored.

(Google, 2015)

So the answer to "can anyone else read my email" is YES. In addition, what this also means is that anyone who sends an email to a Gmail address will also have their email scanned and read, even though they have no connection to Gmail and have not agreed to any of Google's TOS.

This also answers the question about encrypted storage. If "analysis" occurs on stored data, the data must be in cleartext and not encrypted.

In addition, Google's TOS also states:

> When you upload, submit, store, send or receive content to or through our Services, you give Google (and those we work with) a worldwide license to use, host, store, reproduce, modify, create derivative works (such as those resulting from translations, adaptations or other changes we make so that your content works better with our Services), communicate, publish, publicly perform, publicly display and distribute such content.
>
> *(Google, 2015)*

This gives new meaning to the phrase, "don't put anything in an email that you don't want to appear on the front page of the *New York Times*."

From a business perspective, sending business-related information to/from a Gmail account would appear to be less than confidential and a significant security concern.

2.1.3.13 From Outlook.com Privacy Policy

> Microsoft's Outlook.com takes a different approach. From their privacy policy: "We do not use what you say in email, chat, video calls or voice mail to target advertising to you. We do not use your documents, photos or other personal files to target advertising to you.
>
> *(Microsoft, 2015)*

Outlook.com does scan emails for spam, but that appears to be the only use of scanning technology. They specifically state that they do not analyze emails and attachments for advertisement targeting.

2.1.3.14 From Yahoo! Privacy Policy

> ... advertising will be based on our understanding of the content and meaning of your communications. For instance, we scan and analyze email messages to identify key elements of meaning and then categorize this information for immediate and future use.
>
> *(Yahoo!, 2015)*

Yahoo! also scans and uses analytics on email content. We assume this applies to attachments as well, although they do not specifically address this issue.

2.1.3.15 Measures That Can Be Taken to Increase Security and Privacy
To increase the security and privacy of email, the best solution is encryption. This requires encryption key management, which involves key creation, secure key storage, and key distribution. While there are existing solutions for email encryptions, such as PGP, they require a certain degree of technical sophistication that may be beyond many users. Encrypted email only works if the sender and receiver both use the same type of encryption and key management.

2.1.3.16 Conclusion
The three big email services providers, Gmail, Yahoo! Mail, and Outlook.com, provide secure data in motion using HTTPS. They have all updated the way they handle data moving between their data centers by adding encryption. Data at rest is stored unencrypted. There is a data privacy concern given the information that is collect from the user and aggregated with external data. Google and Yahoo! scan and analyze email content passing in and out of their email services, as well as when the email is stored. This applies to emails being sent from any email account into their email systems, which raises privacy concerns. Outlook.com appears to only scan content for viruses.

In the United States email and metadata are subject to civil and criminal litigation. Court subpoenas are required to gain access to email and attachment content. National security letters from a federal agency allows the federal government access to email metadata only; a court order is required for the federal government to access email content. National security letters may prohibit the email service provider from notifying, confirming, denying, or discussing anything about the action.

2.2 CLOUD BACKUP SERVICES

2.2.1 Background
Since the beginning of computing, ensuring the backup and security of data has been vital necessity – a necessity that is often put off until later. A survey conducted by backblaze.com (Back Blaze, 2015) finds that only 6% of users backup their data on a daily basis and that only 13% backup weekly. The survey also found that roughly half of computer owners backup once a year and that 35% have never backed up their computer.

This behavior provides a business opportunity for companies to connect computer users to cloud services. With the advent of high-speed internet and cheap cloud storage, a number of companies now offer inexpensive and automatic file backup. Among the largest and most successful are Carbonite and Mozy. As of 2015, there are at least 50 cloud backup services available, with new ones being started every day. The large internet companies, such as Google, Microsoft, and Amazon are beginning to offer similar services.

Which brings us back to the focus of this book: what are the security and privacy implications of backing up data to the cloud using a service provider?

2.2.2 Case Studies: Comparison of Cloud-Based Backup Security

In this section, we examine security issues of cloud-based data backup. This is done using the case study methodology to illustrate the various security issues when trusting a third party with your data.

2.2.2.1 Questions

Are data in motion and data at rest secure? What is the privacy policy of backup providers? Can the backup provider access the stored data content? If data is encrypted while at rest, who holds the encryption key? Is backup data stored redundantly? Is data stored in multiple locations? Is there physical security of the storage facility(s)? What country(s) are the data stored? Who has jurisdiction? What are the legal issues?

2.2.2.2 Security Concepts

The previously discussed security concepts for data-in-motion and data-at-rest also apply to backup data. That is, data is vulnerable while in transit between the source and destination. In this case between the device containing the data to be backed up and the server where the data is being stored, or backed up to.

For data-in-motion SSL/TLS can be used. HTTPS, which is a higher-level protocol that uses SSL/TLS, is not predominantly used. Instead, the backup service provider uses proprietary software to manage the backup process and implements SSL/TLS as part of its secure transport function.

For backup data storage, encryption is commonly used to ensure that data-at-rest is secure. Since data is being stored in an external location, perhaps several locations, the physical security of the facilities must also be considered as a component to data-at-rest. For example:

- How secure is the facility infrastructure?
- Is the physical structure secure from intruders and natural disasters?
- Is there 24-hour security?
- Who has access to the facility?
- What are the access controls?
- Are employees vetted?
- Is the data in the facility redundantly backed up?
- Are the data centers geographically dispersed?
- What precautions are taken to address cyber-attacks?

2.2.2.3 Methods and Results

To determine the level of security provided by data backup providers, we examine the service providers TOS agreements, privacy policies, and other publically available information.

In this section we evaluate Carbonite and Mozy. These online backup services are accessed through vendor-supplied software or a specialized mobile device app. The service is cloud-based SAAS with files and directory structures stored in the cloud.

2.2.2.4 Carbonite

We begin by analyzing the security of Carbonite backup service from a security perspective by comparing their solution to our security questions.

2.2.2.5 Data-in-Motion

Carbonite addresses data-in-motion security in two ways. First, files are encrypted using 128-bit Blowfish encryption on the host computer containing the files to be backed up, and second they are transmitted to one of their data centers by a proprietary application that uses an SSL connection (Carbonite, 2015). In this case, SSL provides transport encryption to an already encrypted file, which goes beyond the HTTPS data-in-motion security used for browser-based email.

2.2.2.6 Data-at-Rest

Carbonite supports two types of encryption and key control. By default, they create, manage, and securely store the encryption key using Advanced Encryption Standard (AES) 128-bit encryption. Having Carbonite mange the encryption key has several advantages.

First, it frees the user from that task of applying the key to encrypt and decrypt files, and second, the user does not have to ensure the backup and security of the key. This simplifies the sharing of data across devices by leaving the data encryption and decryption process completely up to the management of Carbonite. If data recovery is necessary, the user can access the backed up data using an account username and password. (*Note*: This means that your data is as secure as your password.)

The disadvantage of using the default method is that Carbonite can decrypt your data without your knowledge, although their policy states that they only do this under certain circumstances, such as in response to a court-ordered subpoena.

Carbonite also provides the option for the user to create, control, and manage the encryption key. In this case, backup files are encrypted using AES 256-bit encryption before being moved to Carbonite data centers for storage. The downside of this method is that the user must manage, store, and protect the key. The user supplied private key is also require to restore backed up data.

The advantage of a user-controlled and managed encryption key is that no one at Carbonite can read your data. In response to a court-ordered subpoena, Carbonite can only supply encrypted data. However under court order, you may be required to provide the encryption key.

2.2.2.7 Facility Security
Carbonite describes in their Data Security Practices white paper, the steps that are taken to ensure data security while stored in their facility, which include:

- Climate-controlled data centers
- Redundant power distribution
- Battery backup
- Uninterruptible power supply
- On-site generators with guaranteed fuel contracts
- Data centers are guarded 24 hours a day
- Personnel access to datacenters controlled by biometric scanners and electronic key cards
- Security staff monitoring of all exits to preventing physical theft

- All activity is monitored through closed-circuit television (CCTV).
- Hardened infrastructure protects customers from power loss, weather events, or unauthorized access
- Uses RAID 6 technology to increase data redundancy

Carbonite operates two data centers, both located in Boston. To avoid the single-point-of-failure problem, it is important that data be located in more than one geographic area. While there is a remote chance that an event in Boston could impact both data centers at the same time, the probability is greater than zero. Carbonite's view is that they provide a backup service and there is already geographic redundancy between the user's computer and Carbonite's data center (IT Knowledge, 2009). So if their data centers are unavailable, the user has the original copy. It should also be pointed out that they provide a backup service and not an archive service – Carbonite only keeps backup data for a specified period of time (30 days) after the user deletes it from the user's computer. For a business that depends on data backup/restore availability and continuity of operation, this should be considered when selecting a data backup provider. In addition, data backup and retention policy can have legal and regulatory impact depending on the industry (see Chapter 4 Compliance).

From a legal and jurisdictional perspective, Carbonite is subject to the laws of Massachusetts and the laws of the United States. An in-depth examination of legal issues is provided in Chapter 4.

2.2.2.8 Mozy
In this section we examine another online backup service called Mozy. From a security perspective Mozy has some similarities to Carbonite and some unique features.

2.2.2.9 Data in Motion and at Rest
Like Carbonite, Mozy encrypts each file before it is sent from the user's computer to Mozy's data centers. Data also remains encrypted while stored at the data centers to provide data-at-rest security.

2.2.2.10 Encryption
Mozy uses 256-bit AES keys for encryption, which are created by Mozy's software from a pass phrase entered by the user. This pass phrase is only known to the user and is not shared with Mozy. The user is required to enter this pass phase to access and decrypt

encrypted files when downloading or restoring. It is the user's responsibility to remember the pass phrase. Mozy does not have any knowledge of the pass phrase and therefore cannot decrypt user files if the pass phrase is lost or forgotten.

This is Mozy's default encryption/decryption process – unlike Carbonite which maintains and manages encryption keys by default. From a security perspective, Mozy's default approach is more secure because only the user is able to decrypt backup data: Mozy does not and cannot decrypt data and therefore has no access to data content. It should be stressed that since the user is required to maintain the pass phrase, there is a risk of data loss if the phrase is lost.

Mozy also offers a corporate encryption key option, which uses the same process as previously described, but allows groups to download and decrypt files from backup using a shared key that is used to encrypt/decrypt the 256-bit AES key. This concept allows backups to be shared among multiple users while maintaining the security of the AES key.

Mozy has data centers located in the US, the EU, and across the globe. The main data center is located in Utah, with offices in Pleasant Grove, Utah; London, England; Cork, Ireland; and Shanghai, China – according to their website. There is no specific listing of data center locations. This may be a security precaution. Mozy owned by EMC, a leading provider of storage hardware, and as would be expected, uses EMC products and expertise.

Physical security and polices appear to be state-of-the-art and are similar to those described previously.

Since Mozy stores data in its data centers located in a number of countries, from a legal and jurisdictional perspective, they are subject to the laws of those countries in which they operate. From the information available, data is subject to the laws of the United States and may be subject to the laws of the European Union. In addition, other jurisdictions may be involved including some in Asia, because of their offices in Shanghai, China.

Since Mozy only stores encrypted data and has no access to encryption keys, data content is as secure as the pass phrase used to create the 256-bit AES encryption keys.

2.2.2.11 Privacy
Since the business model of these companies focuses on selling cloud storage, they are not interested in data-mining to sell advertising, as is the case for cloud-based email services. The private information that they collect is used to maintain and grow their businesses, and as such, they have a vested interest securely maintaining the privacy of this information.

2.2.2.12 Conclusion
A number of security issues must be considered when using cloud backup services. Data-in-motion and data-at-rest are handled differently than other cloud services that have been discussed. Data files are encrypted before they leave the user's device. Because data is encrypted before leaving the device and not decrypted until it has been downloaded back to the device, it is as secure as the encryption algorithm, providing a level of security referred to as TNO — trust-no-one.

It is important that data is stored redundantly within a data center and geographically dispersed to maintain the highest level of data security. This is important to guard against natural and man-caused disasters. Jurisdictional issues arise when data is located in multiple states and foreign countries.

2.3 SOCIAL MEDIA

2.3.1 Social Media as Cloud Storage
In this section, we look at social media, cloud storage, and privacy. The goal of social media is to share information with others. Others can be defined as a group of friends, a family, college fraternity, work colleagues, people with similar interests, etc. Social media can also be used to share information and thoughts with everyone anywhere. While information privacy and sharing seem to be at opposite ends of the information security spectrum, we will discuss the intersection and the ramifications of these two qualities on social media.

Twitter and Facebook have been reported to play a key role in social and political movements around the world. As an example, a young underemployed Tunisian college graduate working as a vegetable vendor set himself on fire December 17, 2010, after police stole produce from his stand. This event triggered a revolution in Tunisia that spread across the Arab world, as young Tunisians began organizing on Twitter and Facebook to protest the 23-year regime of President Zine El Abidine Ben Ali. On January 14, 2011, President Ben Ali fled Tunisia, which triggered similar movements across the region from North Africa to Iran.

Another example: On Thanksgiving Day, 2015, several thousand people in Manhattan attempted to disrupt the annual Macy's Thanksgiving Day Parade as part of a protest against a grand jury decision in Ferguson, Missouri. The demonstrators used the hashtag #Stoptheparade on Twitter to rally supporters to their cause.

Interestingly this was first reported in the UK Daily Mail Online with this footer:

Follow us: @MailOnline on Twitter | DailyMail on Facebook

2.3.2 Case Studies: Comparison of Social Media Security (Facebook and Twitter)

Privacy is your right to control personal information and how much you wish to share with others. In this section we analyze privacy policies of Facebook and Twitter as users worldwide share their personal information, thoughts, and observations.

2.3.2.1 Questions

What information is collected? Who is it shared with? What do they do with this data? Where is the data stored? What protections are available?

2.3.2.2 Security Concepts

Previously we discussed data-in-motion and data-at-rest. Since the goal of social media is to share information, motion and rest security are less critical than it is for data backup and cloud-based email. That said, both Twitter and Facebook use HTTPS and SSL to transport data between users and data servers. Data stored in the cloud is not encrypted (*WSJ*, 2013).

The business models of these and other social media companies rely on collecting and aggregating user data to sell advertisements that are targeted to specific user's interests. This allows them to provide a valuable free service, while providing an opportunity to generate revenue.

2.3.2.3 Methods and Results

To address the research questions and privacy versus sharing, we examine Facebook and Twitter's privacy policies, along with other publically available information.

2.3.2.4 Twitter

To help build a more personal Twitter experience for you, we are collecting and occasionally updating the list of apps installed on your mobile device so we can deliver tailored content that you might be interested in.

(Twitter, 2015).

To begin to monetize their product, Twitter is adopting the strategy that has proved effective for Google, Facebook, and others. This requires an update to their privacy policy, which they will provide through an in-app notification on the Twitter app. The update requires the user to take some sort of action within the free Twitter app to opt-out of the new privacy terms of use. The default is opt-in, meaning that by default if you use the app, you agree to Twitter's TOS and privacy policy.

From Twitter's TOS:

What you say on Twitter may be viewed all around the world instantly. You are what you Tweet!

They also state:

The Services that Twitter provides are always evolving and the form and nature of the Services that Twitter provides may change from time to time without prior notice to you.

(2015)

While it is being reported that Twitter will provide you with notification of any change in their TOS, if it is read carefully, the TOS clearly states their service may change without any notification.

The TOS, as is the case of most social media providers, has a reference to the Privacy Policy and states that, "use of the Services you consent to the collection and use (as set forth in the Privacy Policy) of this information, including the transfer of this information to the United States and/or other countries for storage, processing and use by Twitter."

So, by using the service you consent to the collection and use of information generated by you that flows through their system, and that it will be stored in countries all over the world – unencrypted.

In addition, Twitter has the right to provide the information that they collect on you to other companies for syndication, broadcast, distribution, or publication. This is done, because they own data that flows through their system, without any compensation paid to you. If you do not have the right to use the content it may subject you to liability. Of course Twitter will not be held liable, as stated in their privacy policy. This could happen, for example, if a video clip from a cable news program is tweeted, or a picture that is copyrighted by someone else.

They also "reserve the right to access, read, preserve, and disclose any information as we reasonably believe is necessary to (i) satisfy any applicable law, regulation, legal process or governmental request" (Twitter, 2015) that they believe is reasonably necessary. This includes criminal, as well as civil litigation. While this is similar to policies of other social media companies, it must be noted that since Twitter cloud storage and services are located in many countries and jurisdictions, those governments can request and may have access to information that Twitter maintains on their servers about you and your tweets, the people you follow, and the people that follow you. Also "legal process or governmental request" may apply to countries where Twitter does not operate but citizens use Twitter services.

2.3.2.5 Twitter Privacy Policy

Twitter collects personal information during registration that includes name, username, password, and email address. They may also collect the user's phone number if the user wishes to access Twitter using SMS from their cell phone. Other information may be voluntarily given to Twitter and added to the user's public profile, which is *publicly* available. This can include a short biography, your location, your website, and a picture.

As a common practice among social media services, you may choose to upload your email address book to "help you find Twitter users you know or help other Twitter users find you." It also helps the service provider construct social networks that can be valuable when targeting advertising. It can also be used by others, including governments, to determine links between people and organizations.

In their privacy policy, Twitter also states that they broadly and instantly disseminate your public information to a wide range of users, customers, and services, including search engines and publishers that integrate Twitter content into their services. They also make this information instantly available to universities and public health agencies for analysis of "trends and insights." They say this with the well-placed caveat: "you should think carefully about what you are making public."

You may also voluntarily publish location information, which Twitter collects and stores. This includes location information and IP addresses transmitted by your device from cell towers and wireless networks. The privacy implications of collecting and storing location information is that it can be used to find out where you were at specific times in the past and can be used to establish behavioral patterns of movement.

When you interact with Twitter, device and operational information is collected that includes your IP address, browser type, operating system, the referring web page, pages visited, location, your mobile carrier, device and application identifiers, search terms, and cookie information. Twitter also collects information when you use your Twitter account for authentication for access to other services or websites. Also information is collected from websites that you visit that have the Twitter button/widget displayed. There are many websites that display the Twitter button. Few users know that this is a tracking device and that they are being tracked. (*Note*: Facebook and other social media services also use this technique.)

2.3.2.6 Facebook
In this section we look at the security and privacy of Facebook, based on analysis of their current TOS and privacy policy. Once again it must be stated that the purpose of Facebook and other social media services is to share information and once again this information is voluntarily provided by users of the service.

Personal information that users provide when they sign up for Facebook include the user's name, email, gender, and birth date. They are also provided "the opportunity" to add information about where they work, where they went to school, and a photo.

After sign up, people use Facebook to share information about their lives, things they like, photos, videos, links to websites, etc. All of this information can be aggregated and analyzed to form a profile of the user, which can be used to target advertisement.

Facebook provides tools to import email contact lists to help you invite your contacts to join Facebook and add you as a friend. To assist you in this effort, their policy states that, "If you give us your password to retrieve those contacts, we will not store your password after you have uploaded your contacts." They do, however, have access to the uploaded list of contacts.

Similar to Twitter, Facebook collects all of your interactions with their service, your device, network, location, webpages, webpage and cookie information that display the Facebook logo and widget, and browser information. They collect information when you use Facebook for authorization to another website or service. Their TOS also states that, "we may receive a limited amount of information even before you authorize the application or website." What this information is or how it might be used is not defined.

Facebook shares and receives information from advertising partners. The TOS notes that if they receive data that they do not already have they will anonymize the data within 180 days and will stop associating the information with the user. It is not stated what they do with this data during the 180 days.

They collect and aggregate information from other Facebook users about you, such as "when a friend tags you in a photo or video, provides friend details, or indicates a relationship with you."

Photos and videos contain metadata and can provide information about where the picture was taken, when it was taken, latitude/longitude, make and model of the camera, etc. Facebook does not remove this information. They state that if you don't want this information stored, and thus shared, you should remove metadata before uploading. Metadata poses a risk to privacy.

As an example, if you share a picture of your birthday party at your house, metadata could reveal the date and location where the picture was taken. With this information your date of birth and your home location could be determined. Using that information and searching publicly available property records provided by most states and counties in the United States, one could determine when you bought your house, how much you paid for it, the floor plan, and who owns the mortgage if there is one. Then using Google Street View one could "drive" around your neighborhood and see what your house looks like from the street.

The Exchangeable Image File (EXIF) metadata is a standard format that is used for storing information in digital camera/phone image files that use JPEG compression. This metadata can be easily parsed with EXIF viewers and editing tools, such as IrfanView, EXIFtool, and various browser plugins. These tools and others can be used to remove identifying information stored in JPEG images. There are also websites where pictures can be uploaded and the metadata can be viewed, but as you may have guessed, this is another user-generated security risk.

Facebook allows setting restrictions on what is shared. In their privacy settings tab, they have the concept of sharing with "everyone," which means that data is publicly available information, and it may be accessed by everyone on the Internet. Everyone data is subject to indexing by third-party search engines and may be associated with you outside of Facebook when you visit sites on the internet. It may be imported and exported by Facebook and others without privacy limitations. The default privacy setting for certain types of information you post on Facebook is set to "everyone." From a personal privacy perspective, this is a treasure-trove of information that can and will be used by "others" without your permission, because you have agreed to this during sign up.

Facebook provides a way that you can delete "everyone" content that you posted on Facebook, and they will remove it from your Facebook profile. They also state that they have no control over its use outside of Facebook. Deleting information from Facebook does not guarantee that the data does not exist elsewhere on the internet.

Anyone that you make your information available to, which is by default everyone, "may use tools like RSS feeds, mobile phone address books, or copy and paste functions, to capture and export information from Facebook, including your information and information about you."

2.3.2.7 How Facebook Uses Data They Collect

In section 4 of Facebook's Privacy Policy, they describe what they do with the data they collect. "We allow advertisers to choose the characteristics of users who will see their advertisements and we may use any of the non-personally identifiable attributes we have collected (including information you may have decided not to show to other users, such as your birth year or other sensitive personal information or preferences) to select the appropriate audience for those advertisements."

Facebook may display your name and profile photo next to an advertisement displayed to your friends, which may include personally identifiable information. This is the default behavior, but you can choose to opt out.

To supplement your profile, Facebook may collect and aggregate information from your friends. As with other social media providers, Facebook may disclose information pursuant to subpoenas, court orders, or other requests, such as National Security Letters. This applies to criminal matters where they have a good faith belief that the response is required by law. It also applies to civil matters, such as medical malpractice, personal injury, and divorce.

They also state that this may include requests from, "jurisdictions outside of the United States where we have a good faith belief that the response is required by law under the local laws in that jurisdiction, apply to users from that jurisdiction, and are consistent with generally accepted international standards." Privacy and freedom of speech have different meanings in different countries. Know the laws governing the country where you live. The data that you put on Facebook is not private.

By using Facebook you consent to having the information you provide collected and processed in the United States. This makes all users of Facebook subject to the laws of the United States and your data subject to subpoena and National Security Letter actions.

Governments worldwide are requesting user information from Facebook. It is reported that these requests are up by 24% over last six months of 2013. In a report release in 2015, Facebook stated that they received 15,433 US government requests for data associated with 23,667 accounts in the first six months of 2015. They complied with over 80% of the requests (Sci-Tech Today, 2015).

Facebook provides a way to delete an account and the information they have stored on your behalf. However, content that was shared or made available as described in the Privacy Policy may remain viewable and available outside of Facebook.

2.3.2.8 Conclusion

Social media sites like Twitter and Facebook store personal and other data that users voluntarily provide in exchange for using their free service. Their business model relies on using this data to target advertising and for other purposes. These companies, and others, may aggregate user-supplied data with data gathered from external sources to develop a demographic and behavioral profile of users.

Data is subject to legal actions and may be discloses pursuant to subpoenas, court orders, or other requests, such as National Security Letters. Privacy and freedom of speech have different meanings in different countries. Since users and data centers are located globally, requests for data from countries worldwide may be honored. The data that you put on social media is not private. Personal privacy is at risk. Users should consider carefully what they say, upload, and store on social media sites. The only complete privacy protection available is to not use these services.

2.4 OFFICE SUITES

2.4.1 Background

In this section, we look at cloud-based office suites from a security perspective, which includes both analysis of document transport and cloud storage, in addition to data privacy issues.

Both Google Docs and Microsoft 365 are SAAS cloud-based office suites. They provide web-based word processing, spreadsheet, presentation, and drawing applications. They also provide multi-device document storage and sharing through the cloud. Originally these suites where installed on individual computing systems, but with the availability of high-speed internet access, these suites have been moving to the cloud. There are several vendors offering this online capability, and in this section we analyze two of them: Google Docs and Microsoft Office 365 using the case study methodology.

2.4.2 Case Studies: Comparison of Cloud-Based Office Suite Security (Microsoft Office 365 and Google Docs)

2.4.2.1 Questions

Are data-at-rest and data-in-motion secure? Who has access to documents? What are the privacy issues when storing documents in the cloud?

2.4.2.2 Security Concepts

The security concepts for data-in-motion and data-at-rest also apply to office suite documents. That is, data is vulnerable while in transit between the device creating and editing documents and while at rest in the cloud storage facility.

Both Google Docs and Microsoft Office 365 use HTTPS and SSL to secure data-in-motion. They differ slightly in their approach to data at rest. Microsoft charges a monthly or yearly fee to use their service, while Google Docs is free for individual use, Google does charge a fee for business use. As a result their privacy policies differ significantly.

2.4.2.3 Google Docs

Data created in Google Docs is automatically encrypted before it is written to cloud storage and it is automatically decrypted when accessed by an authorized user. Documents and metadata are encrypted with a document-unique key using 128-bit AES encryption. That key is then encrypted with an encryption key associated with the account owner. They keys are additionally encrypted by one of a rotating set of Google's master keys. These encryption keys are created and managed by Google. They provide an option for users to create and manage their own keys.

"Each Cloud Storage objects data and metadata is encrypted with a unique key under the 128-bit Advanced Encryption Standard (AES-128), and the per-object key itself is encrypted with a unique key associated with the object owner. These keys are additionally encrypted by one of a regularly rotated set of master keys. Of course, if you prefer to manage your own."

If the vendor manages the encryption keys they have access to your data. They can be compelled to release encryption keys and encrypted data through court order, subpoena, through government actions, such as through a National Security Letter. To protect data stored in the cloud, encryption must be done on the client side before the document is transported for storage, and the key would have to be unknown to vendor. It must be noted that users are also subject to court orders and subpoenas, which would have the same result and allow data to be decrypted.

2.4.2.4 Privacy
Google treats Google Doc document as content. In their TOS they state that automated systems analyze your content and the results are used for targeted advertising and other purposes as described in Section 2.2. This analysis occurs as the content is sent, received, and when it is stored.

Google also states that by using their service you give Google and their partners a worldwide license to use, host, store, reproduce, modify, create derivative works, communicate, publish, publicly perform, publicly display and distribute content that you create. This includes Google Doc documents.

This stance on privacy is in line with their business model of building user demographic and behavioral profiles to target advertising. The user trades privacy for free access to Google services.

2.4.2.5 Microsoft Office 365
Microsoft encrypts data both at rest and via the network as it is transmitted between a data center and a user. For data at rest Microsoft uses BitLocker 128-bit AES drive encryption to securely store documents in the cloud. BitLocker encrypts the entire storage drive. They also are rolling out per file encryption in the near future (Microsoft, 2015).

2.4.2.6 Privacy
Microsoft takes a different approach to data privacy. They plainly state that they do not mine or access your data for advertising purposes. You own the data you create, process, and store with Microsoft Office 365. It is their policy to not use your data for purpose other than to maintain and provide Office productivity services.

The Office 365 customer owns the data they create, and retain the rights, title, and interest in the data stored in the Office 365 cloud.

2.4.2.7 Conclusion

For both Google Docs and Microsoft 365 data-at-rest and data-in-motion are secure. They use HTTPS and SSL/TLS for transport and both use encryption for data-at-rest. They take different approaches to encryption: Google Docs uses a three-key encryption approach; Microsoft uses whole drive encryption, with individual file encryption being added in the near future.

Google's privacy policy allows them and their partners to scan and analyze documents to build customer profiles. This information is combined with data gathered from other Google services. Profiles are used for target advertising and for other purposes, such as research.

Google's privacy policy gives them and their partners a worldwide license to use, reproduce, create derivative works, publish, and distribute content that you create. Google Docs are not private.

Microsoft's privacy policy takes the approach that your data is yours. They do not use it for target advertising or for any other purpose other than to provide the customers online document creation and storage.

Google Docs is free for consumers; there is a charge for business customers. Microsoft 365 charges both business and consumers for use. They do have a free online version that requires internet connectivity to create and edit documents.

2.5 HEALTH APPS

2.5.1 Background

As people become more health conscience, health and fitness applications (apps) that run on smartphones and tablets have become a growing industry. There are more than 40,000 health-related apps for the Apple iOS iPhone and iPad devices. Similarly there are also thousands of health and fitness apps available for the Android platform. Many of these apps are free or cost a few dollars. The big money driver is in subscription services that provide cloud storage and analysis of the data that is collected, which is reported to be a 4.5-billion-dollar business. This data may also generate revenue by being sold to third parties and data aggregators. With free apps, like free services, read the app's privacy policy before agreeing to the TOS agreement.

2.5.2 Case Studies

In this section we analyze the risks to privacy and security in using health and fitness apps that run on smartphone and tablet platforms. We explore the safeguards, or lack thereof, in the regulatory and medical oversight in the analysis that they provide and in the information that these apps collect.

2.5.2.1 Security Concepts

Health apps, like all other applications which use the cloud for data storage, must implement good security procedures: secure access control, authentication, data-in-motion, and data-at-rest, as previously discussed in this chapter. In addition, there are new wearable devices that collect health information, such as the Apple Watch and other smartwatches. The communication channel between the watch and the smartphone must be secure. Some wearable devices are standalone, which are secure provided that access to the physical device is controlled. Others use Wi-Fi or Bluetooth for communication. Data security using Wi-Fi depends on the security configuration of the Wi-Fi access point. Bluetooth is generally considered to be secure, but recently the security firm Bitdefender demonstrated how Bluetooth communications between Android smartwatches and smartphones could be vulnerable to attacks that can enable the interception of messages and data.

Bluetooth technology uses a secure encryption algorithm to protect data during transmission (data-in-motion) from one device to another. While no wireless technology is completely secure, Bluetooth is reasonably secure for communications. There can be other vulnerabilities in using Bluetooth, such as in the device pairing process.

2.5.2.2 Questions

Is the data collected by health and fitness apps secure in the cloud? What are the risks to privacy? Are there protections and regulations that govern health and fitness data?

2.5.2.3 Efficacy and Oversight

While there are thousands of health and fitness apps, not all of them are big sellers, many are not very useful, and few of them are approved or regulated by the medical profession or a government oversight agency. The few that have been approved are mostly to assist physicians, for example, to allow them to easily share images from X-rays,

CT scans, and cardiac imaging; or used in conjunction with external devices intended for use in diagnosis of specific diseases or conditions. The US Food and Drug Administration's mobile medical app policy does not apply to mobile apps that function as an electronic health record (EHR) system or personal health record system. It therefore is not subject to HIPAA regulations (see Chapter 4 Compliance). The agency does not regulate the sale or general consumer use of smartphones or tablets nor does it regulate mobile app distributors such as the iTunes App Store or the Google Play Store.

The FDA (2015) only focuses its oversight on mobile medical apps that:

• Are intended to be used as an accessory to a regulated medical device – for example, an application that allows a health care professional to make a specific diagnosis by viewing a medical image from a picture archiving and communication system (PACS) on a smartphone or a mobile tablet; or
• Transform a mobile platform into a regulated medical device – for example, an application that turns a smartphone into an electrocardiography (ECG) machine to detect abnormal heart rhythms or determine if a patient is experiencing a heart attack.

The FDA does however encourage the creation and use of health apps that can be used by people to manage their own health and wellness, such as to monitor blood pressure, heart rate, exercise, diet, and caloric intake. The US National Institutes of Health has even created an app called LactMed that provides nursing mothers with information about the effects of medicines on breast milk and nursing infants.

2.5.2.4 Privacy and Security

The main concern from a privacy perspective is what kind of information does the app collect and does it store that information in the cloud. They may collect biometric information, heart rate, blood pressure, etc., or it may be information that the user voluntarily enters, such as diet and exercise routine. It then becomes a question of how secure is the cloud storage, as described in detail in Section 2.3 "Cloud Backup Services." The issues of data-in-motion and data-at-rest, as well as key management and data privacy, are all issues that must be considered. In addition, it must be determined who "owns" the data and who has access to this information. Can the cloud service provider or app developer sell this information to a data aggregator, an insurance company, or a data broker? Answers to these questions can best be determined by a careful review of the app developer and the cloud provider's TOS agreement and their privacy policy.

2.5.2.5 Conclusion

Health data gathered by smartphone apps and stored in the cloud do pose a security risk to individual privacy. For example, health information could have significant monetary value to an insurance company in assessing your health as it determines the cost of both health and life insurance policies. Currently there is no regulation of the data that health and fitness apps collect nor what can be done with the data once it is collected. Most apps are not approved or endorsed by the medical community, and in some instances they may provide false or misleading information. Obviously health decisions are best made in consultation with a physician. That said, health and fitness apps and the data they collect can provide beneficial information that in turn can help us live healthier and longer lives. We must make certain that health-related data is secure when stored using cloud resources to ensure our privacy is preserved.

2.6 SUMMARY

This chapter identifies applications that allow users to store and share data in the cloud. Each section includes case studies of specific categories of applications and associated security considerations. Categories include cloud-based email, backup services, social media, and office suites. Data-in-motion, data-at-rest, and information privacy are discussed using case studies.

REFERENCES

Back Blaze, 2015. 94% of computer users still at risk of data loss. [Online] https://www.backblaze.com/blog/94-of-computer-users-still-risk-data-loss/ (accessed November 2015).

Carbonite Online Backup, 2015. Data Security Practices. [Online] Available from: http://www.carbonite.com/docs/default-source/white-papers/carb-whitepaper-data-security-practices.pdf?sfvrsn=4 (accessed November 2015).

FDA, 2015. US Food and Drug Administration. [Online] http://www.fda.gov/NewsEvents/Newsroom/PressAnnouncements/ucm369431.htm (accessed November 2015).

Google Privacy and Terms, 2015. [Online] Available from: https://www.google.com/intl/en/policies/privacy/#infocollect (accessed November 2015).

GSA, 2015. Rules and Policies - Protecting PII - Privacy Act [Online] Available from: http://www.gsa.gov/portal/content/104256 (accessed December 2015).

IT Knowledge, 2009. Behind the Scenes at Carbonites Backup Service. [Online] http://itknowledgeexchange.techtarget.com/storage-soup/behind-the-scenes-at-carbonites-online-backup-service (accessed November 2015).

Microsoft: Security and Compliance, Office 365, May 2015. [Online] Available from: go.microsoft.com/fwlink/p/?LinkId=401240 (accessed November 2015).

Sci-Tech Today, 2015. Facebook Reports Government Data Requests Rise 24%. [Online] http://www.sci-tech-today.com/news/Facebook--Gov-t-Data-Requests-Up-24-/story.xhtml?story_id=011001 CEOP59 (accessed December 2015).

Twitter, 2015. Terms of Service, [Online] https://twitter.com/tos (accessed December 2015).

UK Guardian, 2015. NSA Surveillance Governmanet Privacy Board Report. [Online] Available from: http://www.theguardian.com/world/2015/jul/02/nsa-surveillance-government-privacy-board-report (accessed November 2015).

US-CERT, [Online] Available from: https://www.us-cert.gov/ncas/bulletins (accessed December 2015).

Wall Street Journal (WSJ), 2013. Digits. [Online] http://blogs.wsj.com/digits/2013/07/31/why-google-doesnt-encrypt-user-data-while-its-stored (accessed November 2015).

Yahoo Privacy Center, 2015. [Online] Available from: https://info.yahoo.com/privacy/sg/yahoo (accessed November 2015).

CHAPTER 3

Privacy Challenges

If a tree falls in the forest and no one hears it, does it make a sound? If someone collects your personal information and it does not harm you, does it matter? Many people consider cloud data security and privacy concerns unnecessary because they believe (1) their data has value only to them, (2) they have herd immunity giving them a low risk, or (3) they have some security protection so attackers will focus on more vulnerable targets. However, more people may covet your data than you think, and more sophisticated tools and computing resources mean more individuals and smaller organizations become low hanging fruit.

We use this chapter to illustrate the scope of privacy issues that might influence the level of security you want for your private cloud data. We will paint a bleak picture intentionally of cloud security and privacy challenges. We hope this will help you make informed decisions about the sensitivity of your data before migrating it to cloud storage.

You represent one of the greatest challenges to your privacy because you decide to put your data in cloud storage. However, those who have information about you can put this data in cloud storage too, and you have less control over this happening. Trust becomes a significant challenge to your privacy.

Both individuals and organizations use private shared cloud storage to share and collaborate with a small trusted group, or to control access to a large number of people. Even private individuals not engaged in commercial activity should exercise some level of data stewardship when it comes to information about others they store in the cloud. Your knowledge of others represents shared information between you and them (Figure 3.1).

You as an individual put your data in the cloud to store or share. You also put information about others in the cloud. You might do this with their knowledge because of some collaborative effort, or without

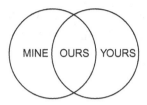

Figure 3.1 Data privacy considerations.

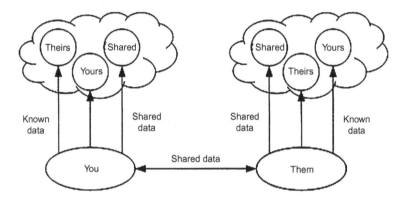

Figure 3.2 Path of private data to the cloud.

conscious thought as part of your own data. Those who know you can do the same with your private data (Figure 3.2).

3.1 WHO WANTS YOUR DATA?

Data privacy challenges exist because your data has value. Figure 3.3 shows just some of the value contained in data that you store in the cloud and make available. Data you store in the cloud might contain, directly or indirectly, a great deal of information others consider valuable. The value could come from the file content itself or from metadata associated with the file, including file access-related data. Figure 3.4 illustrates just some of the individuals and groups who might be interested in the data you store in the cloud.

Your privacy and security considerations should include how others interpret your public cloud data. People often use social media as a diary or chronology of their lives. Companies may also use social media for communication and collaboration internally

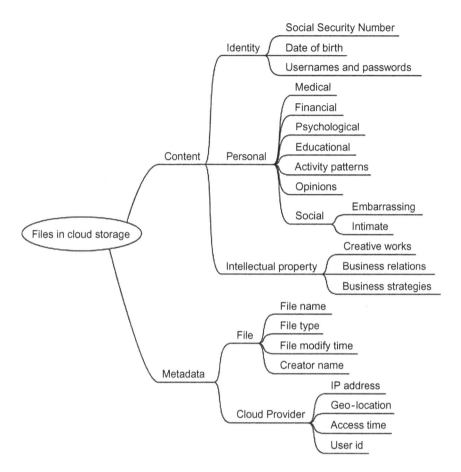

Figure 3.3 The value in your cloud data.

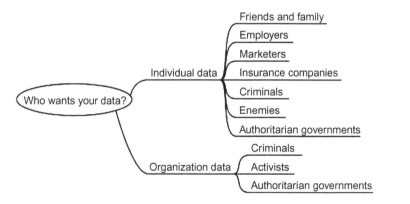

Figure 3.4 Individuals and groups who value your cloud data.

or with clients and partners. Individuals and companies should consider carefully such practices and think about their personal or corporate branding.

Data about individuals stored in the cloud by individuals or by organizations has value to many people. Friends and family would argue they have a legitimate interest in some information. Employers too might want sensitive data about employees, arguing it affects job performance. Marketers obviously seek information to help them segment and predict purchasing decisions. Insurance companies want clues about individual health and lifestyle habits. Criminals use data about individuals for identity theft, cyber-stalking, cyber-bullying, and extortion. Identity thieves might use your identity to establish lines of credit or to conduct illegal activity under an alias. Personal enemies may want information to embarrass or discredit a person. Authoritarian governments want cloud data to identify threats to the status quo.

Organizational data in cloud storage has value for corporate espionage. Competitors can benefit from intellectual property, customer contacts, information about ongoing negotiations, and corporate finances. Activists want organizational data to embarrass or discredit a company. Authoritarian governments might target a foreign organization's cloud storage in retaliation for political challenges (e.g., North Korea and Sony) or to support economic interests in their own country.

Your data has value to many individuals and groups. Now you put that data in cloud storage, in part so it is "always available" on multiple devices no matter where you are. But, if you can get it from anywhere, then others have more opportunities to get it too.

Figure 3.5 shows how both you and others can expose your private cloud data to unintended people and organizations. Cloud providers chosen by you and others can impact your data privacy. Provider terms and conditions, employee actions (mistakes or malice), local laws regarding data privacy in data centers, and cyber-attacks on the provider can result in the loss or exposure of your sensitive data. The practices used by your cloud storage provider for data life-cycle management affect your data privacy. Data retention policies after deletion and not completely erasing data from storage disks in multi-tenant systems can mean your private cloud data persists long after you assumed that it was deleted. This also means that your deleted data is vulnerable.

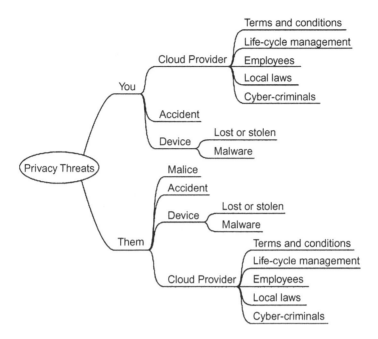

Figure 3.5 Ways to get your cloud data.

The devices that you and others use both hold copies of the data and allow a connection to the cloud storage. Losing control of the device could mean losing control of your private data. You must trust both yourself and others not to make mistakes about security configurations and content. Likewise, you must trust that the people who you share private data with will protect it under all circumstances.

To get an estimate of the value of your data and the ease of obtaining it, we can look at the prices for stolen data and hacking services collected by Dell SecureWorks. The researchers found an uptick in counterfeit documents in 2014. Data collected from various online sites make it easier to obtain or forge such documents. Prices for doxing services (including data collection from social media, public records, social engineering, and installing malware) range from US$25 to US$100. User names and passwords for verifiable online bank accounts cost about 6% of the account value. The price to have a website hacked can cost from US$100 to US$200. Fullz, a complete set of credentials to commit identify theft, typically including full name, address, phone number, email, Social Security Number, bank account and credit card information, sells for US$35−45 (Dell SecureWorks, 2014).

Dell SecureWorks also found the medical and health insurance data can significantly increase the prices for fullz and kitz, which provide everything needed for a complete fake identity. Kitz with verifiable health insurance range from US$1200 to US$1500 each. Fullz with US health insurance sell for around US$500. Health insurance credentials alone (including names, dates of birth, plan information, and insurer contact information for filing claims) have a value of about $20, plus an equal amount for each additional plan like dental or vision (Clarke, 2013).

As for trusting friends and family with your medical and health insurance data, a study by the Ponemon Institute found that victims of medical identity theft more often knew the thief (Ponemon Institute, 2013).

3.2 PRIVACY AND SECURITY INCIDENTS IN THE NEWS

As more sensitive data migrates to cloud storage, we will undoubted hear about more incidents of data breaches. Despite the numerous reports, a recent study (ThreatTrack, 2014) found that a large number of company data breaches go unreported. Companies often do not report data breaches because of concerns about financial or legal consequences. Here we draw attention to some examples that were reported.

The recent health insurance data breach of Anthem, the second largest health insurance company in the United States, could ultimately affect tens of millions of people. The hackers appeared to have used standard phishing and email attachments, some apparently directed at employees with high-level network access, to obtain unencrypted customer data that could complete a fullz. Anthem has agreed to provide two years of identity protection to affected individuals. The burden of what happens after those two years falls on the individual (Hiltzik, 2015).

In 2014, a stolen company laptop with access to the company's cloud storage exposed personnel data including name, address, date of birth, Social Security number, driver's license, and other data (Maryland Attorney General, 2014).

The attack on the Apple iCloud accounts of celebrities in 2014 happened because attackers guessed things like user names, passwords, and answers to security questions (De Looper, 2014).

Residents at a medical university in 2013 used Google Drive and Google Mail for collaborative sharing of patient data. Patient data in the files included patient names, addresses, ages, medical record numbers, dates, provider name, diagnosis, and prognosis (Bowman, 2013).

A virus in 2013 infected cloud data centers of several banks and launched a Distributed Denial of Service (DDOS) attack. This particular virus does not appear to have stolen or destroyed data (Cruz, 2013). However, it does demonstrate that viruses can make their way to cloud providers. Malware that function discretely could steal large amounts of private data before discovery.

Misconfiguration of cloud storage software can result in sensitive data becoming available on the Internet. This happened in 2013 with Amazon S3 (Robertson, 2013). Files and folders in the cloud not properly secured mean anyone on the Internet can potentially get to the data.

A bug in Facebook's "Download Information" in 2013 exposed users email and telephone numbers (Messmer, 2013). Seven years earlier, an obscure bug in server software allowed someone to obtain the names, addresses, birth dates, and Social Security numbers of UCLA students, faculty, and staff (Brooke, 2006). Software security flaws will always put data available from the Internet at risk.

The NSAPRISM (National Security Agency [NSA] Personal Record Information System Methodology [PRISM]) program included the collection of cloud data (Heath, 2013). Ostensibly, the NSA did this to identify terrorist threats. However, some suspect that the NSA also sought cloud data that would give an advantage to economic interests in the United States (Bartlett, 2013).

The examples above show the vulnerability of sensitive data stored in the cloud to stolen devices, bugs in software, viruses, misconfigured security settings, poor passwords, and user errors. Many more examples exist and many more incidence will occur as more individuals and organizations migrate their data to cloud storage. We will also expect to hear about more such incidence if proposed cyber-security legislation becomes law. The proposal includes requirements for data breach reporting by organizations such that they provide a timely notice to their customers who might have had personal data stolen (The Whitehouse, 2015).

3.3 LEGAL ISSUES

We covered in Chapter 2 the many ways that cloud storage provider terms and conditions affect your data privacy. Here we just add a reminder. Your cloud storage provider has expenses paid for by fees to their customers. When you pay for cloud storage you generally have more expectation of data privacy. However, the same does not hold necessarily for free cloud storage. As someone very nicely put, "If you are not paying for it, you're not the customer; you're the product being sold" (Bluebeetle, 2010). This means your data might become a marketing resource for your cloud storage provider to exploit.

Companies that store sensitive customer data in the cloud may find themselves liable for data breaches (Hartwig and Wilkinson, 2014). In Chapter 4 we discuss laws governing such compliance issues for cloud data storage.

In this section we focus on other legal issues for owners of data in cloud storage. We touch on some of the less obvious but important legal implications related to private cloud data.

3.3.1 Travel

Your opinion about data you consider public and private could affect your ability to travel. The United States denied entry to two British tourists who tweeted jokes that US officials considered dangerous (Hartley-Parkinson, 2012). In another case, the UK authorities denied entry to a US man whose website made offensive remarks about women (Calamur, 2014).

The conditions under which law enforcement officials can demand access to your cloud data can vary radically from country to country. For example, Israel security officials routinely demand access to email of those crossing between Israel and the Palestinian Territories. Those that refuse are expelled as terrorists (Russia Today, 2012). Regardless of the need for this level of intrusion without additional supporting evidence, it does illustrate how your private data in the cloud becomes less private when you travel between legal jurisdictions.

3.3.2 Location, Location, Location

Geographic legal jurisdiction has privacy implications. Where your cloud data actually lives might make a difference to your privacy. Recently, a court in the United States ordered Microsoft to provide emails from a customer for a drug investigation. However, the emails existed on Microsoft servers in Dublin, Ireland. Microsoft refused citing privacy and legal jurisdiction of the search warrant. However, a

US court ruled that search warrants for online data actual represent document subpoenas, and determined that Microsoft had to provide the email because they could take the email from the servers in Ireland (Kleinman, 2014).

Regardless of which country you store your online data, if you can get to it then the US government can demand it from you. However, this case shows the possibility that those who store others' data in the cloud could find themselves in a situation where complying with a law in one country results in breaking a law in another country.

3.3.3 Employers and Insurance Companies

Employers have an interest in cloud data of their employees. This data can inform the employer about things employees do or think that could affect the company's reputation, the employee's job performance, or company costs in health insurance. For example, many companies want to charge their employees an extra fee for the higher costs of health insurance (Kingsbury, 2013). Employees may not smoke at work, but shared cloud data in social media could reveal a smoking habit. Even a photo of a rare smoking incident, such as a cigar at a special event, could cast doubt on the employees healthy lifestyle habits.

Insurance companies collect demographic and lifestyle data to build risk profiles of individuals and set their insurance premiums accordingly. Insurance companies can mine public cloud data for information to support not paying a claim or to increase a premium. While understandable from the insurance company perspective, the cloud data owner still has their data used to their detriment and not for the purpose for which they made it available.

Companies have begun offering employees incentives to promote healthy lifestyles, such as fitness tracking devices and programs. These devices collect health data and store it in the cloud (Lazauska, 2013). While voluntary, it does mean employees remain under surveillance by their employers. Furthermore, the devices have little or minimal security. Employers could track employee movement in and out of work, or even check heart rates during meetings to know who feels stressed (Clayton, 2015). Data from your fitness tracking device stored in the cloud could make its way to third-party customers of the cloud provider. Even without your name, an insurance company could combine this data with data from other sources and possibly discover your identity.

3.3.4 Litigation and e-Discovery

Electronic discovery (e-discovery) creates privacy challenges because it must balance the privacy of data owners with legal disclosure laws. Cloud data and international business relations mean e-discovery laws for a particular request may conflict. Agents responsible for collecting and analyzing potential data may not offer the same level of security and privacy as your cloud storage provider, thereby putting your data at risk.

Civil litigation can get nasty, especially divorce cases. Any data that might help the other side will get subpoenaed. Having your data stored in the cloud means you do not have possession of it and the account itself indicates that data of some kind exists and warrants investigation. Your spouse might know or guess your access credentials to your cloud accounts, or install spy software on your devices to obtain data or credentials. In a worst-case scenario, your spouse could delete or upload content to your cloud storage, either of which could create problems for you in court.

3.3.5 Law Enforcement

Moving your data to the cloud where government agencies can analyze it without your knowledge can create problems for you even with a well-intentioned government. A recent ruling by the United States Supreme Court made it clear that a person's Fourth Amendment right does not protect them from search and seizure when law enforcement officials make genuine mistakes about the interpretation of the law (Scocca, 2015). Privacy laws regarding digital media remain ambiguous and inconsistent, so we should expect difficulties because of misinterpretations.

Legal issues exist even when law enforcement authorities obtain data legally. In one case, police used legally obtained data to falsely represent a person online, claiming they could use her data in any way as part of an ongoing investigation. Not only did authorities use the woman's identity, they also used photos of child relatives (Hamby, 2014). This raises the issue of the extent to which authorities can legally manipulate the identity of citizens through control of their social media accounts.

3.3.6 Lifestyle and Psychological Profiling

What are your legal rights when others use information to construct a profile of you as an individual? Marketers do this for targeted advertising, but this does not impose on you any legal obligations or penalties. However, consider the consequences of employers, insurance companies, or law enforcement agencies using your data to build lifestyle and psychological profiles of you.

Companies with access to your cloud data can correlate it with data from other sources and use it to successfully predict such things as pregnancy (Duhigg, 2012). If advertisers can do this, then so can insurance companies. Insurance companies could set the amount you pay based on your lifestyle data from public cloud data sources. Data about your health could come from fitness data collected from devices you wear if terms of service allow.

Researchers like Correa et al. (2010) and Baiet et al. (2012) have begun looking for relationships between social media and the Big Five personality traits, agreeableness, conscientiousness, extraversion, neuroticism, and openness. A recent psychological study found that statistical analysis of Facebook likes produced more accurate personality judgments about people than their friends (Youyou et al., 2015). Employers often give psychological tests to prospective employees. These studies suggest they could do it before even talking to you.

The Philip Dick novel "Minority Report" describes a world where the government pre-convicted people for future crimes based on predictions of possible future behavior. The intent to prevent crime could be used to justify access to all cloud storage data to look for patterns typically seen in those who do commit crimes.

When marketers make a profiling error, you get an irrelevant advertisement. When government agencies make profiling errors, it can cost a person a great deal in time and money to fix the mistake. Consider the cases of people put on no-fly lists for no apparent reason and the difficulties they have in correcting the error (Rath, 2014).

3.4 CRIMINALS, AUTHORITARIAN GOVERNMENTS, AND FRIENDS

Laws of most countries afford individuals and organizations at least some data privacy protections. These laws might seem vague or inconsistent, or offer less than preferred protection. Regardless, some level of data privacy protection exists. Chapter 4 will address compliance and data privacy protection in different countries.

Now we address the non-legal threats to your cloud data. Criminals we know about. However, authoritarian governments with no regard for your right to privacy, or any other right for that matter, pose a serious threat to cloud data security and privacy. Your friends, or the people you trust, often become the greatest source of data privacy breaches.

3.4.1 Criminals

Everyone knows the threat that criminals represent to private cloud data. Criminals have a myriad of ways to get access to your cloud data. They can exploit vulnerabilities in cloud server software, use email phishing attacks to install malware when the recipient opens the attachment, install malware on unattended devices, guess weak passwords, or physically obtain a device able to automatically connect to the cloud storage.

3.4.2 Authoritarian Governments

The recent hack of Sony data related to the movie "The Interview" illustrates several dangers faced by private corporate data. Two main theories exist as to the perpetrators of the Sony hack. The most widely supported suspicion falls on North Korea. However, private security experts think the details of the hack point to a disgruntled employee (Fox News, 2015). The hack resulted in the leak of embarrassing private email exchanges between Sony executives and others, with one top executive ultimately resigning. This attack damaged the public reputations of both a corporation and an individual (Cieply and Barnes, 2015). Regardless of who did it, this example shows the threat to private corporate data from both authoritarian governments and malicious insiders. While not an attack on cloud storage per se, this incident serves to remind us that data stored in the cloud is accessible from anywhere in the world with in Internet connection and becomes a target for those motivated to get it.

We all want to believe that our government will exercise discretion and restraint with respect to data we store in the cloud. That we put this data in a place controlled by a third-party provider should not necessarily leave us out of the loop with respect to permission to access or knowledge of the access.

Many of the documents obtained by WikiLeaks appear to have come from P2P file sharing services. The volume of documents suggests they did not come from a whistle-blower seeking to draw attention to an injustice. Instead, evidence suggests malicious insiders. Even those in the highest levels of the information security business can make mistakes. A Pentagon contractor with top-security security clearance copied sensitive Department of Defense documents to a personal computer that had P2P software installed, resulting in these documents getting leaked (Zetter, 2011).

Unfortunately, not all people live in countries with benevolent governments. Oppressive governments will scan data stored in the cloud for evidence of political dissent. These governments will collect whatever data they can and weave fragments of it together to support their accusations of those who challenge them.

Consider the case of journalist on trial in Egypt. While the Egyptian police got all or most of the data from cell phones and personal computers, and not cloud storage, it does serve to show how making your data easy to get can cause unexpected problems (Kingsley, 2014).

The legal jurisdiction where you use your cloud data storage may not protect you. Your cloud data could even result in harm coming to people in other countries. Consider the Green Movement protests in Iran in 2009. The Iranian government arrested or harassed its citizens who had relatives in other countries who criticized the government on social media (Fassihi, 2009).

3.4.3 Friends

In the category of friends, we must also include you and your family. All of you can put sensitive data at risk in cloud storage.

Most people know not to share Social Security and credit card numbers. However, some people have become victims of fraud because they thoughtlessly posted selfies while holding their first paycheck. Criminals found the images by searching Instagram photos for specific hashtags, then read the account and routing numbers from the images (O'Toole,2014).

You share private information with friends and family, using the cloud to make it available to all from a single place. However, sharing with them means you must trust them to have the same concern for your privacy as you do.

Jeb Bush recently released hundreds of thousands of his emails from his term as Florida governor. These emails contained sensitive information about other people, including their email addresses, home addresses, telephone numbers, Social Security Numbers, and medical information. While the Freedom of Information Act does make the email of public officials part of the public domain, the failure to redact this kind of information does represent a serious data breach, albeit unintended (Sottek, 2015).

Even a prince cannot avoid having damaging data released into the cloud by otherwise friendly people. A woman at a party attended by Prince Harry in Las Vegas took nude photos of him and posted them to Twitter (Robinson and Reynolds, 2012). While apparently not malicious in her intent, the woman clearly did not understand the ramifications of her actions with regard to other people's data in the cloud.

Parents and family members can violate the privacy of children by posting sensitive information or pictures. Sometimes this happens without considering the consequences.

Before the Internet, many children and adults experienced the trauma of having their parents show embarrassing photos to friends who came to visit. Internet social media has the potential to amplify this trauma by exposing the photos to more people and making them harder to forget.

Parents sometimes use social media to punish their children in view of the world. One parent, after catching his young daughter lying about her age, had her wear a shirt with her age and posted the photo to Facebook (Arata, 2014). In another case, parents disciplined their son by posting to Facebook a picture of him dressed as a girl. Authorities brought charges against this couple (WFTV, 2014).

Some parents use social media to discuss medical, psychological, or disciplinary issues with their children. Parents did these things before the Internet. However, social media includes vastly more people in the discussion and effectively leaves a permanent record. Even when laws allow parents to make public sensitive information about their children without consent, parents should consider their children's privacy before sharing information in the cloud.

Parents need to consider the consequences of punishing their children by putting photos and other information about their children on social media. Doing so amplifies the severity of the punishment and may perpetuate it long after its intended duration.

3.5 SUMMARY

Data privacy challenges exist because your data has value to so many, both in the content of the files, the metadata associated with the files, and the identities of those who access the files. Experts expect more incidents of data breaches as more people migrate sensitive data to cloud storage. Using cloud storage to make your data available from anywhere could have legal implications in regard to travel, foreign and domestic laws, employment, and insurance. We all worry about criminals stealing data. However, we should worry equal about ourselves, families, and friends exposing our private data. In the extreme, some must worry about privacy violations by authoritarian governments

REFERENCES

Arata, E., 2014. Dad Makes Sure Boys Know Daughter Is 10 After She Lied About Her Age (Photos). Elite Daily. [Online] 29 October. http://elitedaily.com/news/world/dad-punishes-girl-who-lied-about-age/819687/ (accessed 15.01.15).

Bai, S., Zhu, T., Cheng, L., 2012. Big-Five Personality Prediction Based on User Behaviors at Social Network Sites. Cornell University Library. [Online] 21 April. http://arxiv.org/abs/1204.4809 (accessed 15.01.15).

Bartlett, B., 2013. Is PRISM's "Big Data" about Big Money? The Fiscal Times [Online] 14 July. http://www.thefiscaltimes.com/Columns/2013/06/14/Is-PRISMs-Big-Data-about-Big-Money (accessed 15.01.15).

Beetle, B., 2010. User-driven discontent. MetaFilter [Online] 26 August. http://www.metafilter.com/95152/Userdriven-discontent#3256046 (accessed 15.01.15).

Bowman, D., 2013. Cloud storage debacle marks hospital's third privacy incident in a year. FierceHealthIT. [Online] 30 July. http://www.fiercehealthit.com/story/cloud-storage-debacle-marks-hospitals-third-privacy-incident-year/2013-07-30 (accesses 15.01.15).

Brooke, D., 2006. UCLA Probes Computer Security Breach. The Associated Press [Online] 12 December. http://www.washingtonpost.com/wp-dyn/content/article/2006/12/12/AR2006121200173_pf. html (accessed 15.01.15).

Calamur, K., 2014. U.K. To Deny Entry To Controversial U.S. Dating Guru. National Public Radio (NPR). [Online] 19 November. http://www.npr.org/blogs/thetwo-way/2014/11/19/ 365214976/u-k-to-deny-entry-to-controversial-u-s-dating-guru (accessed 15.01.15).

Cieply, M., Barnes, B., 2015. Amy Pascal Lands in Sony's Outbox. New York Times [Online] 5 February. http://www.nytimes.com/2015/02/06/business/amy-pascal-leaving-as-sony-studio-chief. html (accessed April 2015).

Clarke, E., 2013. Hackers Sell Health Insurance Credentials, Bank Accounts, SSNs and Counterfeit Documents, for over $1,000 Per Dossier. Dell SecureWorks. [Online] 15 July. http:// www.secureworks.com/resources/blog/general-hackers-sell-health-insurance-credentials-bank-accounts-ssns-and-counterfeit-documents/ (accessed April 2015).

Clayton, N., 2015. Office fitness trackers: Fun perk or creepy leash? BBC News. [Online] 6 January. http://www.bbc.com/capital/story/20150105-fitness-freebie-or-big-brother (accessed 15.01.15).

Correa, T., Hinsley, A.W., De Zuniga, H.G., 2010. Who interacts on the Web?: the intersection of users' personality and social media. Comput. Hum. Behav. 26 (2), 247–253.

Cruz, X., 2013. Hacked through the Clouds. Cloud Times [Online] 23 February. http://cloud-times.org/2013/02/23/hacked-through-the-clouds/ (accessed 15.01.15).

Dell SecureWorks, 2014. Underground Hacker Markets. [Online] December. http://www.secure-works.com/assets/pdf-store/white-papers/wp-underground-hacking-report.pdf   (accessed   April 2015).

De Looper, C., 2014. Cloud hacking isn't as hard as most would think. Tech Times [Online] 3 September. http://www.techtimes.com/articles/14800/20140903/cloud-hacking-isnt-hard-think. htm (accessed 15.01.15).

Duhigg, C., 2012. How Companies Learn Your Secrets. New York Times Magazine. [Online] 16 February. http://www.nytimes.com/2012/02/19/magazine/shopping-habits.html   (accessed 15.01.15).

Fassihi, F., 2009. Iranian crackdown goes global. Wall Street J. [Online] 3 December. http:// www.wsj.com/articles/SB125978649644673331 (accessed 15.01.15).

Fox News, 2015. FBI director reveals new evidence linking N. Korea to Sony hack, answers skeptics. Fox News. [Online] 7 January. http://www.foxnews.com/politics/2015/01/07/fbi-director-reveals-new-evidence-linking-n-korea-to-sony-hack-answers-skeptics/ (accessed 15.01.15).

Hamby, C., 2014. Government Set Up A Fake Facebook Page In This Woman's Name. BuzzFeed News. [Online] 6 October. http://www.buzzfeed.com/chrishamby/government-says-fed-eral-agents-can-impersonate-woman-online (accessed 15.01.15).

Hartley-Parkinson, R., 2012. "I'm going to destroy America and dig up Marilyn Monroe": British pair arrested in U.S. on terror charges over Twitter jokes. Daily Mail. [Online] 31 January. http://www.dailymail.co.uk/news/article-2093796/Emily-Bunting-Leigh-Van-Bryan-UK-tourists-arrested-destroy-America-Twitter-jokes.html (accessed 15.01.15).

Hartwig, R.P., Wilkinson, C., 2014. Cyber Risks: The GrowingThreat. Insurance Information Institute. [Online] June. http://www.iii.org/sites/default/files/docs/pdf/paper_cyberrisk_2014.pdf (accessed 15.01.15).

Heath, N., 2013. PRISM fallout could cost US cloud industry billions, warns Europe's digital chief. ZDNet. [Online] 7 July. http://www.zdnet.com/article/prism-fallout-could-cost-us-cloud-industry-billions-warns-europes-digital-chief/ (accessed 15.01.15).

Hiltzik, M., 2015. Anthem is warning consumers about its huge data breach. Here's a translation. Los Angeles Times. [Online] 6 March. http://www.latimes.com/business/hiltzik/la-fi-mh-anthem-is-warning-consumers-20150306-column.html (accessed April 2015).

Kingsbury, K., 2013. Your Company Is About to Get a Lot More Interested in Your Waistline. Reuters. [Online] 13 November. http://www.dailyfinance.com/2013/11/13/company-health-insurance-penalties-smoking-obesity-obamacare/ (accessed 15.01.15).

Kingsley, P., 2014. Australian journalist accuses Egyptian prosecutors of unbelievable inefficiency. The Guardian. [Online] 22 May. http://www.theguardian.com/world/2014/may/22/australian-journalist-al-jazeera-egyptian-prosecutors-unbelievable-inefficiency (accessed 15.01.15).

Kleinman, Z., 2014. Tech rivals join Microsoft in fight over US data demand. British Broadcasting Company (BBC). [Online] 16 December. http://www.bbc.com/news/technology-30494562 (accessed 15.01.15).

Lazauska, J., 2013. How A Virtual Fitness Plan Pushed 300 Coworkers To Lose Weight. Forbes. [Online] 1 August. http://www.forbes.com/sites/centurylink/2013/08/01/how-a-virtual-fitness-plan-pushed-300-coworkers-to-lose-weight/ (accessed 15.01.15).

Maryland Attorney General, 2014. Maryland Information Security Breach Notices – 2014, Case Number 237729. Maryland Attorney General. [Online] http://www.oag.state.md.us/idtheft/breachNotices2014.htm (accessed 15.01.15).

Messmer, E., 2013. 12 of the worst data breaches of 2013 so far. Network World. [Online] 18 July. http://www.networkworld.com/article/2291388/security/111254-12-of-the-worst-data-breaches-of-2013-so-far.html (accessed 15.01.15).

O'Toole, J., 2014. #StealMyIdentity: Fraudsters use paycheck selfies to steal bank details. CNN Money. [Online] 29 October. http://money.cnn.com/2014/10/29/technology/social/instagram-identity-theft/ (accessed 15.01.15).

Ponemon Institute, 2013. 2013 Survey on Medical Identity Theft. [Online] 11 September. http://www.ponemon.org/blog/2013-surveyonmedical-identity-theft (accessed April 2015).

Rath, A., 2014. Hard-To-Change Mistakes Led To Successful "No-Fly List" Case. National Public Radio (NPR). [Online] 29 June. http://www.npr.org/2014/06/29/326718019/hard-to-change-mistakes-led-to-successful-no-fly-list-case (accessed 15.01.15).

Robertson, J., 2013. How Private Data Became Public on Amazon's Cloud. Bloomberg. [Online] 27 March. http://www.bloomberg.com/news/2013-03-26/how-private-data-became-publiconamazon-s-cloud.html (accessed 15.01.15).

Robinson, M., Reynolds, E., 2012. Well, they do call it close protection: Prince Harry pictured in Las Vegas pool party jacuzzi with a VERY relaxed bodyguard (who failed to stop girl taking naked snaps). Daily Mail. [Online] 27 August. http://www.dailymail.co.uk/news/article-2194207/Intimate-pictures-Prince-Harrys-wild-weekend-Vegas.html (accessed April 2015).

Russia Today, 2012. Israel bars activist as "terrorist" for refusal to open e-mail. Russia Today. [Online] 5 June. http://www.rt.com/news/israel-e-mail-tamari-doughman-004/ (accessed 15.01.15).

Scocca, T., 2015. Supreme Court: It's OK for Cops to Guess Wrong About What the Law Is. Gawker. [Online] 15 December. http://gawker.com/supreme-court-its-ok-for-cops-to-guess-wrong-about-wha-1671321023 (accessed 15.01.15).

Sottek, T.C., 2015. Jeb Bush dumps emails including social security numbers of Florida residents online. The Verge. [Online] 10 February. http://www.theverge.com/2015/2/10/8013531/jeb-bush-florida-email-dump-privacy (accessed April 2015).

The White House, 2015. Securing Cyberspace - President Obama Announces New Cybersecurity Legislative Proposal and Other Cybersecurity Efforts. The White House, Office of the Press Secretary [Online] 13 January. https://www.whitehouse.gov/the-press-office/2015/01/13/securing-cyberspace-president-obama-announces-new-cybersecurity-legislat (accessed April 2015).

ThreatTrack Security, Inc, 2014. Malware Analysts Have the Tools to Defend Against Cyber-Attacks, But Challenges Remain. ThreatTrack Security, Inc. [Online] http://www.threattracksecurity.com/resources/white-papers/cyber-attacks-internal-challenges-malware-analysts-face.aspx (accessed 15.01.15).

WFTV, 2014. Police: Mom posts pics of son dressed as girl on Facebook as form of discipline. WFTV. [Online] 12 December. http://www.wftv.com/news/news/local/police-mom-posts-pics-son-facebook-dressed-girl-fo/njRSJ/ (accessed 15.01.15).

Youyou, W., Kosinski, M., Stillwell, D., 2015. Computer-based personality judgments are more accurate than those made by humans. Proceedings of the National Academy of Sciences, Early Edition. [Online] 7 January. http://www.pnas.org/content/early/2015/01/07/1418680112.short (accessed 15.01.15).

Zetter, K., 2011. Claim: WikiLeaks Published Documents Siphoned Over File Sharing Software. Wired. [Online] 20 January. http://www.wired.com/2011/01/wikileaks-and-p2p/ (accessed April 2015).

CHAPTER 4

Compliance

For businesses, the cloud offers significant advantages in terms of flexible and inexpensive storage. By offloading the everyday operation, maintenance, backup, and disaster recovery takes to cloud service providers, companies can realize substantial cost savings not only in terms of hardware and software licenses, but also in reduced labor costs and facility expenses. In addition, cloud solutions also offer the ability to dynamically scale capacity to meet business cycle and future growth requirements at a predictable cost.

But, and there is always a but, if an entity, business or individual, is subject to laws and regulation regarding data storage and transmittal, those regulations also apply to the cloud service provider. It is up to the business that outsources their storage to a cloud provider to ensure that the provider meets regulations that are prescribed by the governing law. When data is entrusted to a cloud storage provider, due diligence must be taken to ensure legal and regulatory compliance.

4.1 LEGAL RESPONSIBILITY WHEN HANDLING OTHER PEOPLE'S DATA

There are a number of state and federal laws and regulations that must be considered when moving data to the cloud. What laws apply depends on the type of business and the type of data that the business collects, stores, and maintains. The majority of these laws focus on the protection of personally identifiable information (PII).

The National Institute of Science and Technology (NIST) defines PII as, "any information about an individual maintained by an agency, including (1) any information that can be used to distinguish or trace an individual's identity, such as name, social security number, date and place of birth, mother's maiden name, or biometric records; and (2) any other information that is linked or linkable to an individual, such as medical, educational, financial, and employment information" (NIST, 2015).

Note that this definition uses the word "agency" and is intended primarily for US federal government agencies, but other organizations may find the definition useful.

Examples of PII include, but are not limited to:

- Name, such as full name, maiden name, mother's maiden name, or alias
- Personal identification number, such as social security number (SSN), passport number, driver's license number, taxpayer identification number, or financial account or credit card number
- Address information, such as street address or email address
- Personal characteristics, including a photographic image (especially of the face or other identifying characteristics), fingerprints, handwriting, or biometric data (e.g., retina scan, voice signature, facial geometry)
- Information about an individual that is linked or linkable to one of the above (e.g., date of birth, place of birth, race, religion, weight, activities, geographical indicators, employment information, medical information, education information, financial information).

The US federal government has enacted a number of laws that regulate the collection, transmittal, storage, and maintenance of PII. Many states have also enacted state laws that impact storage and use of PII. While these laws focus mainly on specific business sectors, such as the healthcare and financial industries, services provided by cloud storage providers must adhere to the same laws and regulations as the businesses that use them for storage of PII.

This section will focus on four US federal laws that govern or impact data storage in the cloud. These include:

HIPAA – The Health Insurance Portability and Accountability Act of 1996 establishes federal standards for protecting patients' health information. Entities that have access to medical data are required to protect the privacy of patient information by adhering to prescribed guidelines.

Dodd-Frank – The purpose of the Dodd-Frank Wall Street Reform and Consumer Protection Act is to "promote the financial stability of the United States by improving accountability and transparency in the financial system, to end 'too big to fail', to protect the

American taxpayer by ending bailouts, to protect consumers from abusive financial services practices, and for other purposes" (Dodd-Frank, 2010). To achieve these goals, organizations must collect, store, maintain, and provide search capabilities for all communication records relating to transactions.

GLBA – The Gramm–Leach–Bliley Act, also known as the Financial Services Modernization Act of 1999, requires financial institutions to establish standards for protecting the security and confidentiality of customer non-public personal information.

SOX – The Sarbanes-Oxley Act of 2002, also known as the Public Company Accounting Reform and Investor Protection Act, was established to regulate the financial practices of US public companies to protect against fraud. Part of the SOX Act directly affects data storage that includes the preservation and accuracy of electronic records, the recommended retention period for record storage, and the types of business records that SOX rules apply to, which includes all communications.

4.2 US FEDERAL LAWS AND REGULATIONS AFFECTING CLOUD STORAGE

Each of the four acts are discussed in this section as they apply to cloud storage. None of the four actually prescribe specific solutions to address the requirements, nor do they endorse or recommend any vendor's approach. Instead, they provide "guidelines," leaving the actual implementation to the regulated entities to allow them to take advantage of current and future technology.

4.2.1 HIPAA

As previously stated, the Health Insurance Portability and Accountability Act of 1996 establishes federal standards for protecting patients' health information. Entities that have access to medical history, such as doctors, dentists, hospitals, and health insurance companies, are required to protect the privacy of patient information by adhering to prescribed guidelines (HIPAA Health Insurance Reform: Security Standards; Final Rule, 2003).

The law requires that any entity possessing Protected Health Information (PHI) must "protect against reasonably anticipated threats to the security or integrity of the information," according to the US Department of Health and Human Services. Note that PHI and PII are similar in that they refer to an individual's private data. PHI extends that concept to include medially related information, such as lab results, diagnosis, treatments, medications, and prescriptions. There is no official HIPPA certification for business entities, including cloud storage providers. The current best practice is to provide authorization and access controls, and to encrypt data in motion and at rest. It is "felt" that adopting these best practices helps address the obligation to protect storage of PHI.

There are four areas of HIPAA that directly impact the storage of PHI in the cloud:

- Policy – Establish access control policies, procedures, and technology to restrict access to PHI by authorized personnel only
- Physical Security – Control physical access to areas where PHI is stored
- Technical Security – Implement technical security mechanisms, such as encryption, to protect PHI data in motion and at rest
- Backup – Establish appropriate data backup, disaster recovery, and emergency operation strategies

HIPAA applies to "covered entities," which is defined as (1) health plans, (2) health care clearinghouses, and (3) health care providers who electronically transmit any health information. These entities are bound by the privacy standards even if they contract with others organizations, called "business associates" to perform some of their essential functions. The law does not give the Department of Health and Human Services (HHS) the authority to regulate other types of private businesses or public agencies through this regulation. For example, HHS does not have the authority to regulate employers, life insurance companies, or public agencies that deliver social security or welfare benefits.

Most health care providers and health plans outsource some of their health care activities and functions. They often use the services of other persons or businesses. The HIPAA privacy rule requires that a covered entity obtain satisfactory assurances from its business associates that the associate will appropriately safeguard the PHI it receives or creates on behalf of the covered entity. These assurances must be in writing, whether in the form of a contract or other agreement between the covered entity and the business associate.

Cloud service providers are considered business associates under the HIPAA privacy rules. A covered entity's contract with its business associate must:

- Describe the permitted and required uses of PHI by the business associate.
- Provide that the business associate will not use or further disclose PHI other than as permitted or required by the contract or as required by law.
- Require the business associate to use appropriate safeguards to prevent use or disclosure of PHI other than as defined in the contract.

If a covered entity knows of a breach or violation by the business associate of the contract, the covered entity is required to take reasonable steps to remedy the breach or end the violation, and if such steps are unsuccessful, to terminate the contract with the business associate.

HIPAA specifies the overall general requirements for covered entities as it pertains to protecting PHI. These are followed by a set of administrative and technical requirements, which can be either required or addressable. If an implementation specification is described as "required," the specification must be implemented. The concept of "addressable implementation specifications" was developed to provide covered entities additional flexibility with respect to compliance with the security standards. In meeting standards that contain addressable implementation specifications, a covered entity must do one of the following for each addressable specification:

- Implement the addressable implementation specifications
- Implement one or more alternative security measures to accomplish the same purpose
- Not implement either an addressable implementation specification or an alternative

The covered entity's choice must be documented. The covered entity must decide whether a given addressable implementation specification is a reasonable and appropriate security measure to apply within its particular security framework. This decision will depend on a variety of factors, such as the entity's risk analysis, risk mitigation strategy, what security measures are already in place, and the cost of implementation. The decisions that a covered entity makes regarding addressable specifications must be documented in writing. The written documentation should include the factors considered, as well as the results of the risk assessment on which the decision was based (HHS, 2014).

4.2.1.1 General Requirements

HIPAA defines general requirements for creating, storing, maintaining, and using PHI. The covered entity must ensure the confidentiality, integrity, and availability of all PHI data that is received, maintained, or transmitted, and must be protected against any "reasonably anticipated threats or hazards" to the security or integrity of the information.

Covered entities must also protect against any "reasonably anticipated" uses or disclosures of such information that are not permitted or required under HIPAA, and must ensure the compliance by its workforce. This implies that there is a training program and that employees, and business associates, are trained in handling PHI.

There is some flexibility to the approach taken to meet the requirements of protecting PHI, as defined by HIPAA. Covered entities may use any security measures that "reasonably and appropriately" implement the standards and specifications defined by HIPAA.

In deciding which security measures to use, a covered entity must take into account the following factors:

- The size, complexity, and capabilities of the covered entity
- The covered entity's technical infrastructure, hardware, and software security capabilities
- The costs of security measures
- The probability and criticality of potential risks to the PHI

4.2.1.2 Administrative Safeguards

Administrative safeguards define the policies and processes that need to be in place to protect PHI. A covered entity must have a management process to handle PHI that implements policies and procedures to prevent, detect, contain, and correct security violations. A data backup plan is required that establishes and implements procedures to create, maintain, and restore exact copies of PHI information. A disaster recovery plan is also required, along with procedures, to restore PHI in the event of a natural or man-made disaster and to ensure against any loss of data.

An emergency mode operation plan is also required that establishes and implements procedures to enable continuation of critical business processes for protection of the security of PHI data while operating in emergency mode. Emergency mode operating must be periodically tested and revisions to contingency plans updated as necessary, this includes both supporting applications and PHI data.

4.2.1.3 Technical Safeguards

Technical safeguards are defined in HIPAA that address access controls, data in motion, and data at rest requirements. A covered entity must implement technical policies and procedures for computing systems that maintain PHI data to restrict access to only those persons that have been granted access rights. Each user is required to have a unique user identification (ID). This ID is used for identifying and tracking the activities of the user while accessing PHI. Audit controls must be implemented to record and provide the ability to examine PHI access and processing activity. To protect the user account from being left unattended, automatic logoff must be implemented to terminate a user's session after a predetermined time of inactivity.

HIPAA requires that a mechanism to encrypt and decrypt PHI must be implemented. It does not directly specify when data is to be encrypted/decrypted, except when it is "reasonable and appropriate" to do so. Given this flexibility, PHI should be encrypted while in motion and at rest. Encryption directly addresses the data *confidentiality* requirement of PHI as is transmitted, received, maintained, and stored. The selection of an encryption algorithm, implementation details, and use are left to the covered entity.

To ensure PHI data *integrity*, the covered entity must implement policies and procedures to protect PHI from improper alteration or destruction. It must also establish emergency access procedures for obtaining and accessing PHI during an emergency (HIPAA 164.312 Technical Safeguards, 2003).

The Department of Health and Human Services developed a security matrix that provides an overview of HIPAA security requirements. It also has references to specific sections of the law that provide detailed information. Appendix A to Subpart C of Part 164—Security Standards: Matrix is shown in Table 4.1.

Table 4.1 Appendix A to Subpart C of Part 164 – Security Standards: Matrix

Standards	Sections	Implementation Specifications (R) = Required, (A) = Addressable	
Administrative Safeguards			
Security Management Process	164.308(a)(1)	Risk Analysis	(R)
		Risk Management	(R)
		Sanction Policy	(R)
		Information System Activity Review	(R)
Assigned Security Responsibility	164.308(a)(2)		(R)
Workforce Security	164.308(a)(3)	Authorization and/or Supervision	(A)
		Workforce Clearance Procedure	(A)
		Termination Procedures	(A)
Information Access Management	164.308(a)(4)	Isolating Health care Clearinghouse Function	(R)
		Access Authorization	(A)
		Access Establishment and Modification	(A)
Security Awareness and Training	164.308(a)(5)	Security Reminders	(A)
		Protection from Malicious Software	(A)
		Log-in Monitoring	(A)
		Password Management	(A)
Security Incident Procedures	164.308(a)(6)	Response and Reporting	(R)
Contingency Plan	164.308(a)(7)	Data Backup Plan	(R)
		Disaster Recovery Plan	(R)
		Emergency Mode Operation Plan	(R)
		Testing and Revision Procedure	(A)
		Applications and Data Criticality Analysis	(A)
Evaluation	164.308(a)(8)		(R)
Business Associate Contracts and Other Arrangement	164.308(b)(1)	Written Contract or Other Arrangement	(R)
Physical Safeguards			
Facility Access Controls	164.310(a)(1)	Contingency Operations	(A)
		Facility Security Plan	(A)
		Access Control and Validation Procedures	(A)
		Maintenance Records	(A)
Workstation Use	164.310(b)		(R)
Workstation Security	164.310(c)		(R)
Device and Media Controls	164.310(d)(1)	Disposal	(R)
		Media Re-use	(R)
		Accountability	(A)
		Data Backup and Storage	(A)

(Continued)

Table 4.1 (Continued)			
Standards	**Sections**	**Implementation Specifications (R) = Required, (A) = Addressable**	
Technical Safeguards			
Access Control	164.312(a)(1)	Unique User Identification	(R)
		Emergency Access Procedure	(R)
		Automatic Logoff	(A)
		Encryption and Decryption	(A)
Audit Controls	164.312(b)		(R)
Integrity	164.312(c)(1)	Mechanism to Authenticate Electronic Protected Health Information	(A)
Person or Entity Authentication	164.312(d)		(R)
Transmission Security	164.312(e)(1)	Integrity Controls	(A)
		Encryption	(A)

4.2.2 Dodd-Frank

The purpose of the Dodd-Frank Wall Street Reform and Consumer Protection Act is to "promote the financial stability of the United States by improving accountability and transparency in the financial system to protect the American taxpayer by ending bailouts, to protect consumers from abusive financial services practices, and for other purposes." To achieve these goals, organizations that are subject to this Act must collect, store, maintain, and provide search capabilities for all communication records relating to transactions. This includes electronic mail, instant messages, and recordings of telephone calls, both fixed line and mobile phones.

It requires that records of all communications that relate to each transaction, regardless of the medium, must be stored. They must be able to be retrieved in a way that allows the reconstruction of the communication, both pre- and post-trade, and keep all records together with all pertinent data and memoranda.

Record retention varies based on record type. Since transactional records provide trade-related information, retention requirement is set to the life of a swap, plus 5 years. For voice communication, the retention period is 1 year. For non-transactional records, retention is set to 5 years from the moment record was created. Since financial instruments can last for many years, as in the case of long-term bonds, the aggregate retention period could conceivably extend up to 30 years (ndm.net, 2013).

Originally, the Commodity Futures Trading Commission (CFTC) was very specific in the type of medium that could be used for storing records. They leveraged a previous rule, which was in existence before Dodd-Frank. This rule mandates use of Write Once Read Many (WORM) compliant medium for storing records. This type of storage includes devices where information can only be written once and cannot be modified, such as optical disk technology like DVD-ROM and CD-ROM. This requirement was problematic for financial institutions and current cloud technology vendors. While optical disk storage is a well-known technology, it is also an old technology that does not scale well, poses physical storage and management problems, and does not easily allow for current state-of-the-art large-scale searching solutions.

Appeals were made to the CFTC by interested parties and the language was later amended in 2013 to remove WORM-related language so as not to specify a solution or media type. This type of specificity of technology is usually not found in major laws. The new language specifies the intent of the law, that is, data is to be protected from modification or deletion for a specified period of time.

From the new ruling: "A broker-dealer would not violate the requirement in paragraph (f)(2)(ii)(A) of the rule if it used an electronic storage system that prevents the overwriting, erasing or otherwise altering of a record during its required retention period through the use of integrated hardware and software control codes. Rule 17a-4 requires broker-dealers to retain records for specified lengths of time. Therefore, it follows that the non-erasable and non-rewriteable aspect of their storage need not continue beyond that period."

As the law was originally written, cloud storage using magnetic media hard drives would not meet the intent of the law, but with the modification to rule 17a-4, organizations that fall under Dodd-Frank can store records in the cloud if the proper safeguards are in place. Given these special requirements, cloud vendors are coming up with various methods to ensure that their solution prevents the overwriting, erasing, or otherwise alteration of a record during its retention period.

From a security standpoint, the Dodd-Frank law is mostly concerned with data integrity, retention, and availability. If a cloud solution is used, it must ensure that data integrity is maintained and that data cannot be altered, erased, or overwritten. Availability can be achieved using standard cloud storage techniques, such as backup, striping, and load balancing.

In addition, the rules specify that all records must be maintained in a manner that is easily searchable, which implies that record data is not encrypted, at least at some point, to facilitate searching. Although there are techniques that can be used to search encrypted data, Dodd-Frank does not appear to require that level of confidentiality.

The single most important capability that is required by Dodd-Frank is the ability for trade reconstruction. Cloud solutions can provide this capability by implementing comprehensive trade reconstruction, which addresses the recordkeeping requirements.

The challenges for a Dodd-Frank cloud solution are (1) ensuring data integrity, (2) providing search capabilities of all records, (3) identifying and collecting the required data, (4) efficiently organizing data storage, and (5) implementing comprehensive trade reconstruction.

4.2.3 Gramm–Leach–Bliley Act

The Gramm–Leach–Bliley Act (GLBA), also known as the Financial Services Modernization Act of 1999 is commonly pronounced "glibba," was enacted on November 12, 1999. It requires financial institutions to establish standards for protecting the security, integrity, and confidentiality of their customers' nonpublic personal information. Nonpublic personal information (NPI) is any "personally identifiable financial information" that a financial institution collects about an individual in connection with providing a financial product or service, unless that information is otherwise publicly available. Section 501(b) of the act specifies the objectives of these standards:

- The Financial Privacy Rule – secure the privacy of customer information and records
- The Safeguards Rule – provide ongoing protection against threats to the security and integrity of customer information

- The Pretexting provisions – prevent unauthorized access and use of customer information by accessing private information using false pretenses (e.g., phishing, social engineering)

The law covers a broad range of financial institutions, including many companies not traditionally considered financial institutions because they engage in certain "financial activities." The privacy rule applies to businesses that are "significantly engaged" in "financial activities" as described in section 4(k) of the Bank Holding Company Act. This can include banks, lenders, check cashers, wire transfer services, sellers of money orders, credit counselors, financial planners, tax preparers, accountants, and investment advisors, loan brokers and services, debt collectors, real estate settlement services, and others (FTC, 2015).

GLBA guidelines direct financial organizations to "evaluate" the use of encryption to secure customer information while in motion and at rest. The Federal Financial Institutions Examination Council is a formal interagency body of the US government made up of five banking regulators, including the Federal Reserve Board of Governors, and others, that is "empowered to prescribe uniform principles, standards, and report forms, and to promote uniformity in the supervision of financial institutions" (FFIEC, 2014). The council stated that financial institutions should employ encryption to mitigate the risk of disclosure or alteration of sensitive information in storage and transit, and they should utilize effective key management practices to protect encryption keys.

GLBA prohibits the sharing of certain kinds of customer financial information with unaffiliated parties. A cloud storage company may be considered an unaffiliated party so the encryption of customer information should be done prior to being transmitted to the cloud provider for storage. Some cloud providers allow customers, in this case the financial institution, to provide and manage their own encryption keys. This would meet the intent of GLBA if the encryption is done prior to leaving the financial institutions premises and the cloud provider does not have access to the key; otherwise there is a possibility that cloud provider employees could access covered data. Encryption of data prior to transfer also addresses the risk of disclosure or alteration of sensitive information in transit, although most if not all cloud storage service providers use SSL for data in motion.

Additionally, GLBA requires that financial institutions give customers written privacy notices that explain their information-sharing practices.

> Information on the content of the notification, who should receive it, how often, opt-out requirements, etc. can be found at http://www.ftc.gov.

4.2.4 SOX

The Sarbanes-Oxley Act (SOX) of 2002, administered by the Securities and Exchange Commission (SEC), was established to regulate the financial practices of companies and protect against fraud. The bill was enacted as a reaction to a number of major corporate and accounting scandals, including Enron, and WorldCom. Many publicly held companies and registered public accounting firms come under the jurisdiction of SOX, which defines a set of standards and guidelines for how data should be stored, accessed, and managed.

Section 802 of Sarbanes-Oxley describes three areas that affect the management of electronic records, which impact cloud storage:

1. Protection of records from destruction, alteration or falsification
2. Retention period for record storage
3. Types of information that need to be stored that includes all business records and associated communications

Section 802 of the act states that a company is responsible for any financial misconduct, even if it is the fault of a third party. If a company is subject to SOX regulation, then this requirement also flows down to their subcontractors and service providers, which would include cloud service providers. This implies that the service providers must have the necessary processes and controls in place to ensure SOX compliance. In order to help determine compliance, a set of auditing standards, called the SSAE 16, has evolved.

The Statement on Standards for Attestation Engagements No. 16 (SSAE 16) is an attestation standard put forth by the Auditing Standards Board (ASB) of the American Institute of Certified Public Accountants (AICPA) that can be used to evaluate internal control over financial reporting. The SSAE 16 standard is a report that states that a company has the proper internal controls and processes for the type of information and transactions it handles.

The SSAE 16 SOC 2 report is based on trust service principles (SSAE-16, 2015), which are defined as:

- The *security* of a service organization's system.
- The *availability* of a service organization's system.
- The processing *integrity* of a service organization's system.
- The *confidentiality* of the information that the service organization's system processes or maintains for user entities.
- The *privacy* of personal information that the service organization collects, uses, retains, discloses, and disposes of for user entities.

For cloud providers, having SSAE 16 SOC 2 certification is an industry standards-based approach to address SOX compliance.

4.3 CLOUD STORAGE PROVIDER AND COMPLIANCE

The four laws that were discussed in Section 4.2 all have similar intent, that is, to protect private information and in some cases to ensure that information is not lost or corrupted. Cloud storage provides an excellent solution to addresses many of the concerns that are described in these regulations as it pertains to data security, integrity, confidentiality, availability, redundancy, and disaster recovery. Implementation details are left to the regulated entity and their subcontractors and business associates. In all cases, any organization that has access to protected data is subject to rules and regulations described in the governing Act(s). In addition, businesses that use cloud services must have contracts or agreements with cloud third parties that include wording to ensure that the service provider is in compliance with regulations and requirements of applicable laws.

Using industry best practices for meeting these requirements is a good starting point. The HIPAA Security Standards Matrix, shown in Table 4.1, provides an outline of security standards for administrative, physical, and technical safeguards. While this specifically applies to HIPAA, the areas discussed have applicability to meeting the intent of the other regulatory Acts.

Encryption of information in motion and at rest is specifically discussed in several Acts that were discussed. Encryption is also provided by the majority of cloud providers. But it cannot be emphasized strongly enough, that encryption is only as secure as the password or pass-phase that controls the encryption key, and is only as secure as the people entrusted to maintain and access the key.

If the cloud provider encrypts data at rest, but controls the key to encrypt and decrypt the data, the storage of PII does not meet the intent of the law. One way to address this issue is for the covered entity to encrypt the PII before it leaves its network to be stored at the cloud provider's location. Since the PII is encrypted prior to transfer, the cloud service provider does not have access to PII – they only have random encrypted bits. This requires the covered entity maintain and control access to the encryption key.

As described in the section on HIPAA, the covered entity is responsible for the actions of their business partners, including cloud service providers. In the case of HIPAA, a special contract is *required* between the covered entity and the cloud provider that spells out the security requirements for managing and storing PHI. These security requirements must meet HIPAA standards. If the cloud provider is a qualified business associate and implements the security requirements defined by HIPAA, then it is possible that the cloud storage provider could manage the encryption key(s) and still be in compliance with HIPAA regulations.

Another way that PII can be protected is to remove any identifying information from the PII before it is transferred and stored. While this is possible, it may not meet the requirements of SOX and Dodd-Frank which require complete transactional records to be kept. De-identified PII is often used for research in health care and for other government statistical purposes. HIPAA has a provision for a limited data set, from which most but not all potentially identifying information has been removed.

4.4 LAWS AND REGULATIONS OF OTHER COUNTRIES

So far we have focused on the laws of the United States that govern data that is stored in the cloud. Other countries have passed laws to protect the privacy of their citizens. With the Internet and multi-national companies that have worldwide data storage facilities, the idea of borders and jurisdictions become complicated. While countries can pass laws to protect their citizens' privacy, it is difficult in the current environment to keep data from crossing borders and being used for whatever purpose. What is unlawful in one country may be perfectly legal in another. This section will provide an overview of some of those laws and provide references to more detailed information.

4.4.1 European Data Protection Directive of 1995

The European Data Protection Directive of 1995 was created to ensure that data are protected in the same manner throughout the European Union. This provides a framework and a set of principles to assist in data-related compliance for companies doing business with countries in the EU. Rather than having to navigate the data regulatory laws of 28 different EU countries, companies doing business in the EU would have a single source to ensure compliance. The directive also expands the rights of the individual to be informed of the types of data that is collected and challenge the way this data are handled. The individual has the right to know which government agencies have access to which kind of personal data.

This directive was agreed to by EU members in 1995. That was in the pre-dawn of the Internet and decades before the concept of cloud computing and storage and did not anticipate or accommodate technological changes and developments such as data globalization, social networks, and cloud computing. As a result, the European Commission determined that new guidelines for data protection and privacy were needed. The commission has set forth a set of proposals for a comprehensive reform of the Data Protection Directive that updates and modernizes the principles defined in the 1995 Directive.

The European Commission defines personal data as "any information relating to an individual, whether it relates to his or her private, professional or public life. It can be anything from a name, a photo, an email address, bank details, and posts on social networking websites, medical information, or a computer's IP address." The reforms are summarized in the EU Commission's fact sheet (EU Commission, 2012).

4.4.1.1 Benefits for EU Citizens

The data protection reform will strengthen citizens' rights and thereby help restore trust. Better data protection rules mean you can be more confident about how your personal data is treated, particularly online. The new rules will put citizens back in control of their data, notably through:

- **A right to be forgotten:** When you no longer want your data to be processed and there are no legitimate grounds for retaining it, the data will be deleted. This is about empowering individuals, not about erasing past events or restricting freedom of the press.

- **Easier access to your own data:** A right to data portability will make it easier for you to transfer your personal data between service providers.
- **Allowing you to decide how your data is used:** When your consent is required to process your data, you must be asked to give it explicitly. It cannot be assumed. Saying nothing is not the same thing as saying yes. Businesses and organizations will also need to inform you without undue delay about data breaches that could adversely affect you.
- **The right to know when your data has been hacked:** For example, companies and organizations must notify the national supervisory authority of serious data breaches as soon as possible (if feasible within 24 hours) so that users can take appropriate measures.
- **Data protection first, not an afterthought:** "Privacy by design" and "privacy by default" will also become essential principles in EU data protection rules – this means that data protection safeguards should be built into products and services from the earliest stage of development, and that privacy-friendly default settings should be the norm – for example, on social networks or mobile apps.

4.4.1.2 Benefits for Business

Data is the currency of today's digital economy. Collected, analyzed and moved across the globe, personal data has acquired enormous economic significance. According to some estimates, the value of European citizens' personal data has the potential to grow to nearly €1 trillion annually by 2020. Strengthening Europe's high standards of data protection is a business opportunity. The European Commission's data protection reform will help the digital single-market realize this potential, notably through four main innovations:

- One continent, one law: The Regulation will establish a single, pan-European law for data protection, replacing the current inconsistent patchwork of national laws. Companies will deal with one law, not 28. The benefits are estimated at €2.3 billion per year.
- One-stop-shop: The Regulation will establish a "one-stop-shop" for businesses: companies will only have to deal with one single supervisory authority, not 28, making it simpler and cheaper for companies to do business in the EU; and easier, swifter, and more efficient for citizens to get their personal data protected.

- The same rules for all companies – regardless of their establishment: Today European companies have to adhere to stricter standards than companies established outside the EU but also doing business with the Single Market. With the reform, companies based outside of Europe will have to apply the same rules. We are creating a level-playing field.
- European regulators will be equipped with strong enforcement powers: data protection authorities will be able to fine companies who do not comply with EU rules with up to 2% of their global annual turnover. The European Parliament has even proposed to raise the possible sanctions to 5%. Privacy-friendly European companies will have a competitive advantage on a global scale at a time when the issue is becoming increasingly sensitive.

The updates, as described in the fact sheet, have not been adopted yet. The Commission's proposals, once the details have been agreed to, will be passed on to the European Parliament and EU Member States, meeting in the Council of Ministers, for discussion. It is expected that these changes to the Directive will be adopted by the end of 2015 or early 2016. The updated directive will take effect 2 years after it is adopted.

What does this mean for cloud storage security and privacy? As we discussed in Chapter 2, the terms of service and privacy policies of "free" services require that users give up private information in exchange for free services, such as those provided by Google, Yahoo!, Twitter, and others. While these services do require that the user provide "explicit" consent when agreeing to the use of their private data, and they do inform the users as to what they will do with their data, the concept of the "right to be forgotten" is not addressed.

The right to be forgotten has implications to both citizens and to companies doing business in the EU. Even before the updated directive is issued, lawsuits have been brought against data companies based on the existing directive from 1995 and subsequent modifications. Google was sued in EU court by a Spanish citizen who wanted the Google search engine to delete personal information about him that stems from an auction notice of his repossessed house in 1998. The case worked its way to the top European court where Google was ordered to delete "inadequate, irrelevant or no longer relevant" data from its results when a member of the public requests it. Strangely, the site that hosts the information can continue to make the information available.

A Google spokesperson said: "The ruling has significant implications for how we handle takedown requests. This is logistically complicated not least because of the many languages involved and the need for careful review. As soon as we have thought through exactly how this will work, which may take several weeks, we will let our users know."

As of May 2014, more than 247,000 requests "to be forgotten" were received by Google based on the European ruling (Google).

While this ruling focused on links to outdated data, the proposed changes to the EU Directive could have far reaching consequences for data collectors, social media services, free services, cloud providers, data aggregators, etc. As pointed out in Chapter 2, many companies make their money by collecting and selling personal data for targeted advertising. This data is collected, aggregated, combined with public information, and sold many times over. Imagine what it would take to accomplish this request from a single individual: "I am exercising my right to be forgotten, please remove any and all data that pertains to me."

4.4.2 United Kingdom's Data Protection Act 1998
While the EU Data Protection Directive aims at providing a unified standard for data protection and regulation across Europe, many European countries have their own laws and regulations in place.

The United Kingdom's Data Protection Act 1998 and subsequent amendments is how the United Kingdom implements the European Directive. The purpose of the Act is to protect the rights and privacy of individuals and to ensure that data about them is processed only with their knowledge and consent. The Act gives individuals certain rights regarding personal information held about them and places certain obligations on those who process the personal information. Like the EU Directive, the Act defines two distinct groups: data controllers – those that process information and data subjects – those whose data are subject to processing.

4.4.2.1 Data Protection Principles
These obligations are defined in a set of eight Data Protection Principles (GOV.UK, 2014). Data controllers must ensure that information is:

- Used fairly and lawfully.
- Used for limited, specifically stated purposes.
- Used in a way that is adequate, relevant and not excessive.

- Accurate.
- Kept for no longer than is absolutely necessary.
- Handled according to people's data protection rights.
- Kept safe and secure.
- Not transferred outside the UK without adequate protection.

There is stronger legal protection for more sensitive information, such as:

- Ethnic background
- Political opinions
- Religious beliefs
- Health
- Sexual health
- Criminal records

The Data Protection Act gives you the right to find out what information the government and other organizations stores about you. The organization is legally required to give you a copy of the information they hold about you if you request it. There are some situations when organizations are allowed to withhold information, e.g., if the information is about:

- The prevention, detection or investigation of a crime.
- National security or the armed forces.
- The assessment or collection of tax.
- Judicial or ministerial appointments.
- An organization does not have to say why they are withholding information.

4.4.2.2 Regulation and Enforcement
The regulation and enforcement of the Act is the responsibility of the Information Commissioners Office (ICO). The ICO provides guidance to organizations and individuals and has various rights of enforcement against data controllers who do not comply with the Act. If a data subject feels that a data controller has not complied with the Act then the data subject has:

- The right to ask the ICO to investigate non-compliance.
- The right to sue the data controller.

The Act also treats it as a criminal offence if:

- A data controller having received a subject access request destroys the data rather than disclose it.

- A data subject does not comply with an enforcement notice.
- A data subject knowingly or recklessly obtains, discloses or procures the disclosure of personal information without the consent of the data controller.

4.4.3 India — Information Technology Act 2000 (IT Act)

The basic regulations governing information technology in India are defined in the Information Technology Act of 2000, and subsequent amendments and clarifications of the law. It is commonly referred to as the IT Act (India IT Act, 2008).

There are two sections of India's IT Act that address personal privacy, which has an impact on cloud storage. Section 43A of the IT Act provides for the protection of sensitive personal data. In the United States this type of data would be called personally identifiable information (PII). Companies and organization that process and/or store PII must implement and maintain "reasonable security practices and procedures." If data handlers do not implement these security best practices and procedures and as a result causes "wrongful loss or wrongful gain to any person," it may be required to pay damages.

The IT Rules, outlined under section 43A of the IT Act, define "reasonable security practices and procedures" that must be implemented, and what constitutes "sensitive data and information." The IT Act and the IT Rules regulate the collection and use of sensitive personal information.

The Indian government has also proposed specific legislation on privacy beyond the current IT Rules, called the Privacy Bill, which enhances an individual's right to privacy. In the bill, individual privacy rights cannot be infringed except for:

- Protection of India's sovereignty or integrity.
- National security.
- Prevention of commission of crime.
- Public order.

Unauthorized collection, processing, storage, and disclosure of personal information are treated as infringement of privacy under the Privacy Bill.

- A data controller discloses personal data without the authority to do so.

4.4.3.1 Sensitive Personal Data

Under the IT Act sensitive personal data means any personal information that the government considers as such, and does not have a specific definition. Currently, the IT Rules consider sensitive personal information as relating to:

- Medical records and history.
- Physical, physiological and mental health condition.
- Biometric information.
- Financial information such as bank account or credit card details.
- Passwords.
- Sexual orientation.

In general, personal information has been considered to mean any information that is capable of identifying an individual person directly, indirectly or in combination with other information. This goes to the heart of the business models of data collectors and aggregators that use such information for targeted advertising and personal profiling. Publically available information is not considered personal information and is not protected under the IT Rules.

One interesting exemption in the IT Rules is that the collection and disclosure of sensitive personal information does not apply to data collected by *data processors* that collect information on behalf of *data controllers*. What this means is that if a Company A (data controller) outsources data collection to Company B (data processor), Company B is exempt from the IT Rules provisions dealing with collection and disclosure of sensitive personal information; which somewhat makes sense in that Company B is disclosing information to Company A.

4.4.3.2 Privacy Policy Compliance

Data processors and controllers must have defined privacy policies and practices, which must be made easily available to individuals when data is being collected. Policies must identify what data is being collected, why the data is being collected, and how the data will be used. It must also define the conditions under which the information will be disclosed. I addition, the policy must define the security practices and procedures that are implemented to ensure confidentiality of information. Before data is collected, the consent must be obtained from the individual. Consent must be explicitly expressed and cannot be implied.

4.4.3.3 Security Policy Compliance

The security policy of data controllers and processors must define the physical, technical, operational, managerial, and security control measures that are appropriate for the sensitivity of the information being protected. The IT Rules state that the ISO/IEC 27001 standard for information management (ISO/IEC 27001, 2013) can be implemented to ensure data security. Different standards can be used, provided they are approved by the government of India. Compliance with these standards must be audited and certified annually by government-approved agencies.

4.4.3.4 Regulation and Enforcement

The Indian government in 2011 clarified that the IT Rules only apply to corporations and persons located in India. The IT Rules do not apply to foreign corporations or persons located outside India, or when information is collected from persons located outside India. There are no national regulators dealing with enforcement of privacy laws. To date, there have been no reported cases alleging a breach of privacy under the IT Act or the IT Rules.

4.5 SUMMARY

This chapter examined cloud storage with respect to four US federal laws and regulations that govern industries that might benefit from the advantages offered by cloud storage providers. Four governing laws were examined:

- Health Insurance Portability and Accountability Act – health care
- Dodd-Frank Wall Street Reform and Consumer Protection Act – accountability and transparency of the financial system
- Gramm–Leach–Bliley Act – customer protection in financial institutions
- Sarbanes-Oxley Act – corporate disclosures

In addition, overviews of data protection laws from countries other than the United States were discussed. From a cloud storage perspective, these laws outline security measures that must be in place to protect personal information. Whether it is referred to as Personally Identifiable Information (PII), Protected Health Information (PHI), or Nonpublic Personal Information (NPI), the security requirements are similar. Their goals are to ensure the security, integrity, confidentiality, and availability of information. Industry best practices provide a starting point for achieving these goals that include administrative, physical, and technical safeguards.

Please note: this chapter is provided for information purposes only and is not, nor is intended to be, legal advice.

REFERENCES

Dodd-Frank, 2015. [Online] Available from: http://www.cftc.gov/lawregulation/doddfrankact/index.htm (accessed January 2015).

EU Commission, 2012. [Online] Available from: http://europa.eu/rapid/press-release_IP-12-46_en.htm (accessed May 2015).

FFIEC, 2014. [Online] Available from: http://www.ffiec.gov (accessed January 2015).

FTC, 2015. [Online] Available from: http://www.ftc.gov, 2015 (accessed January 2015).

Google [Online] Available from: https://www.google.com/transparencyreport/removals/europe-privacy/?hl=en (accessed May 2015).

GOV.UK, 2014. [Online] Available from: https://www.gov.uk/data-protection (accessed May 2015).

HHS - Department of Health and Human Services, 2014. [Online] Available from: http://www.hhs.gov (accessed January 2015).

HIPAA, 45 CFR Parts 160, 162, and 164 Health Insurance Reform: Security Standards; Final Rule, 2003. [Online] Available from: http://www.hhs.gov/ocr/privacy/hipaa/administrative/securityrule/securityrulepdf.pdf (accessed January 2015).

HIPAA, 164.312 Technical Safeguards, 2003. [Online] Available from: http://www.hhs.gov/ocr/privacy/hipaa/administrative/securityrule/securityrulepdf.pdf (accessed January 2015).

IndiaITAct, 2008. [Online] Available from: http://www.deity.gov.in/content/information-technology-act (accessed May 2015).

ISO/IEC 27001, 2013. [Online] Available from: http://www.iso.org/iso/home/standards/management-standards/iso27001.htm (accessed May 2015).

Meet your Dodd-Frank recordkeeping compliance requirements, 2013. [Online] Available from: http://www.ndm.net/archiving/pdf/Dodd-Frank%20recordkeeping%20compliance%20requirements.pdf (accessed January 2015).

NIST, 2015. Guide to Protecting the Confidentiality of Personally Identifiable Information (PII) [Online] Available from: http://csrc.nist.gov/publications/nistpubs/800-122/sp800-122.pdf (accessed January 2015).

SSAE-16, 2015. [Online] Available from: http://www.ssae16.org (accessed January 2015).

CHAPTER 5

Privacy Tools

This chapter reviews several methods and tools to enhance data privacy and security.

You should think of the cloud storage provider's FAQ as the first tool in securing your data. There, you will find instructions to best use the provider's storage service to protect your private data. In the FAQ, look for a mention of the provider's data center locations if you believe legal jurisdiction may affect your data privacy.

This chapter provides a discussion of the types of additional privacy protection to supplement or replace that offered by your cloud storage provider. These tools can complement your existing cloud data storage security, or serve as alternatives if you cannot find a cloud storage provider that meets your data privacy needs. We mention specific products and companies to give examples of the kinds of privacy tools available. These mentions do not reflect endorsements of these products or companies. Only you can make such judgments about your data privacy requirements. Use the information here as a starting point for your own privacy tool investigations and evaluations.

5.1 TWO-FACTOR AUTHENTICATION

Two-factor authentication makes your mobile device a tool to protect the privacy of your cloud data. Two-factor authentication requires you to initiate a login to your cloud storage account with a user name and password. Next, a one-time passphrase is sent to your mobile device to complete the login process.

This second step of the two-factor authentication supports data privacy in two ways. First, attempts by attackers to access your cloud data online will fail because the attackers do not have the final passphrase unless they have also obtained your mobile device. Second, you will receive notification of any attempts to access your cloud data storage account. In the worst case, attackers might guess the one-time phrase and gain access to your data, but it is highly unlikely. However, two-factor authentication will at least alert you to the attack.

Two-factor authentication does have a drawback in that it requires having your mobile device with you when you access your data. This can be a problem if you forget or lose your device, someone steals it, or the battery has no charge. Data could be stored in multiple locations, but storing or caching your private data in multiple places means you have multiple issues to consider for keeping it secure.

Small companies and organizations that share data via commercial providers like Google Drive and Dropbox can require two-factor authentication for their employees and customers to access data. This solution requires coordination (and trust!) of all parties involved to ensure they do in fact have two-factor authentication on their accounts that they use to access shared data.

Alternatively, companies and organizations may want to use a private cloud and host the data themselves. Again, they might use two-factor authentication or provide some other secure interface to the cloud data. For these options, they will need to (1) configure their web server to generate one-time passwords and (2) provide a mechanism for users to also generate the same password. There are commercial products available to facilitate this option. This solution requires some upfront costs for setup and maintenance by the IT department.

One simple solution for two-factor authentication has the server pre-generate a list of passwords and this printed on a piece of paper and given to the user. Each time the user logs in, s/he uses the next password. While simple, this implementation has problems with running out of passwords before the user gets a new set, losing the paper with the passwords, and having the passwords unknowingly copied and used by an unauthorized user.

The Google Authenticator solves these problems by providing a client application that generates the same time-based one-time password (TOTP) as the server. Google has an Apache server module to provide this capability through the PAM authentication framework (Price, 2015). This solution does not scale well for large numbers of users, frequent adding and removing of user accounts, and support for handling authentication problems. However, it does provide a reasonably inexpensive and straightforward way to secure cloud data for a small, stable group of people (Duckett, 2012).

5.2 ENCRYPT YOURSELF

You can protect the privacy of your cloud data by encrypting data yourself before storing it to the cloud. This approach protects data in transit and at rest. Your cloud provider only stores the data that you encrypt and that you control. You do not upload unencrypted data and have your cloud storage provider encrypted it when it arrives. It also means you control the encryption password and/or encryption keys.

Cloud storage providers that offer "client-side" encryption might still have access to your password and encryption keys, or may provide actual zero-knowledge encryption. Unfortunately some of the encryption password generation schemes used by cloud providers have predictable patterns that attackers can discover and exploit. Disadvantages of encrypting data yourself means (1) you have to do it, probably in a separate step from uploading or downloading, (2) you must manage and protect passwords and keys, which can become complicated if you choose to share data.

Encrypting data yourself before storing it to the cloud allows you (1) to use unencrypted cloud storage, (2) to avoid sending the cloud storage provider unencrypted data for them to encrypt and possibly data mine, and (3) to avoid trusting zero-knowledge encryption.

Zero-knowledge encryption may have flaws in the implementation that make it possible for the provider or others to predict the password or encryption keys. Zero-knowledge encryption may not apply when you share your data. In such cases, your unencrypted data may exist at least temporarily with the cloud storage provider.

CipherApps (http://www.cipherapps.com/) provides real-time secure collaboration of Google documents and sheets. CipherApps uses zero-knowledge encryption to encrypt files saved to your Google Drive through their web interface.

EncFS (https://vgough.github.io/encfs/) makes it possible to create encrypted user-space file system rooted at an arbitrary directory. A separately named mount point allows users an unencrypted view of the files. To use EncFS to secure your cloud data, create a directory for

EncFS in your local cloud storage directory (e.g., Dropbox or Google Drive), then use a mount point outside the cloud storage directory.

Boxcryptor (https://www.boxcryptor.com/) implements EncFS for Windows. Boxcryptor uses a random AES key to encrypt the file and the public RSA keys of those with permission to view the file to encrypt this file encryption key. Boxcryptor then uploads both the encrypted file and encrypted file key(s) together in cloud storage.

You can roll your own encrypted file system with an encrypted archive file. On your local machine you have the directory tree you want encrypted. Use an archive tool like 7-Zip (http://www.7-zip.org/) to create an encrypted archive of this file and upload this encrypted archive to your cloud storage.

5.3 SECURE EMAIL FOR CLOUD STORAGE

People often use their email accounts to store data and files that they can retrieve later or from another device. People might also use the same email account to share information and collaborate, either by sending email only to themselves or by saving messages as drafts. Private data can exist in the email message body or in attached files. While this method has an email interface, it has the same fundamental issues associated with explicit cloud data storage. You must protect the data in transit to and from the email account, as well as at rest on the email server.

Email providers may offer some kind of encryption to users. However, in many cases the email provider controls the encryption keys. Just as with secure cloud storage, this means you must trust the ability and intentions of the provider to value your data privacy as much as you. ProtonMail (https://protonmail.ch/) provides a zero-knowledge email encryption service. In addition, they have their data center in Switzerland so your email data falls under Swiss Federal Data Protection Act (DPA) and the Swiss Federal Data Protection Ordinance (DPO).

Email clients with public key encryption capabilities offer another way to have private email messages. The Scribe email client works on both Linux and Windows and has a GnuPG plugin (http://www. memecode.com/scribe/gnupg.php). The Enigmail (https://www.enigmail.net/) extension to Thunderbird and SeaMonkey provides public key encryption of email messages.

5.4 PASSWORDS AND ENCRYPTION KEYS

Passwords and public key encryption provide the foundation for data privacy by encrypting your data and controlling access to your cloud storage account. Attackers can apply brute force password attacks to cloud data accounts, and then apply this same technique to the encrypted data files themselves. If they gain access to the key stores then they can work offline to crack the key store encryption. They can also seek to obtain the private key needed to decrypt any encrypted files they acquire. Thus, the password and private key store become the private data of most security concern.

Several password generation tools exist to reduce your risk of brute force password attacks on your cloud data accounts and on encrypted data files themselves. People choose passwords they can easily remember, perhaps with the idea that it makes it more secure because they do not have to write it down.

However, easily remembered often means easily guessed. A variety of strategies exist to make complex but easy to remember passwords by combining words and numbers and applying patterned substitutions. Unfortunately, if you can apply a rule to create a password, then so can a password cracker. Any rule you can think of probably has already become part of a password cracking tool.

The following suggestions will help with your password generation and management:

- Use long, random passwords.
- Use unique password for each site.
- Change the password frequently and unpredictably. Allied intelligence broke the encryption of the Enigma machine because the Nazis did not change the password frequently enough (Bletchley Park).

Consider using a password manager to create and manage passwords for you. You need to remember one very secure password to access the password manager. The password manager generates long, random passwords for you and will usually handle account logins automatically.

LastPass (https://lastpass.com/) works as a browser plugin and provides limited file sharing for a fee. LastPass will synchronize your key store across all your devices so you can access your accounts from anywhere. LastPass also offers enterprise single-sign-on (SSO) products and services. KeePass (http://keepass.info/) runs from a USB stick and has features to protect against keystroke loggers and caching. KeePass will periodically delete passwords from the clipboard, but this remains a vulnerability when using untrusted computers. 1Password (https://agilebits.com/onepassword) offers yet another popular solution for password management. Finally, security expert Bruce Schneier designed the password manager Password Safe (http://pwsafe.org/).

As your password manager master password, you might consider generating and memorizing a random 14-character long password of 26 English language letters, including capitals, and the digits 0−9. A brute-force attack on such a password will take the current fastest supercomputer about 4500 years to break. Even with rapid supercomputing technology advances, your private data will likely remain private or will no longer have value to you or anyone else by the time the encryption gets cracked.

You can generate random passwords using the aforementioned password managers. Alternative, you can use an online random password generator, such as from LastPass (https://lastpass.com/generate-password.php). For true randomness, change the default "Minimum Digit Count" from 1 to 0. Memorize the password you generate by breaking it into chunks for 3−4 characters. Alternative, create a memorable phrase from your password (not vice versa!) by choosing words that begin with the characters in the password. For example, the password "xPgpbSGIdj5zac" could become "Xander, Please get peanut butter Sandwich Glue. I did join 5 zoos and churches."

Practice learning your password by typing it into a document. This will help build muscle memory and engage more of your brain to aid learning. If you want to test your memory of the password before going live with it on an actual account, save the document using this password and try opening it in a day or two. Save a document with a password in most office suites by "File-Save As" and check "Save with password." If you forget the password when you come back to the document later, just delete the document and start over. When you feel confident that you have memorized the password, use it as your master password with your favorite password manager or use it with you cloud storage account.

5.5 PAY FOR SECURITY

Many cloud data storage providers offer encryption and other privacy enhancements for paid accounts. Paying for cloud data security makes your private data less likely to become the providers product. You will most likely have to pay for additional security if you are a business that is subject to federal regulations such as HIPAA, as discussed in Chapter 4.

However, data privacy issues remain. You still must depend on the cloud storage provider to manage its own security. Furthermore, if the provider manages the encryption keys then local laws governing the data centers where your data resides might allow access to your unencrypted data without the due process you expect in your own legal jurisdiction. Furthermore, local laws might place restrictions on the type of encryption used. Such situations might arise in countries that provide at least tacit support for industrial espionage or oppose political activism, just to name a few.

If you do pay for additional security, consider insisting on zero-knowledge encryption. Zero-knowledge encryption means that your data gets encrypted before it uploads to the cloud storage provider. The provider does not know your encryption key and cannot help you decrypt data if you forget or lose your key. Without zero-knowledge encryption, a third party has the keys to your private data. By contract, they agree not to use these keys to view your data. However, the legal system exists in part because people break contracts and these third parties might fall victim to a data breach.

Mega (https://mega.co.nz/), SpiderOak (https://spideroak.com/), Tresorit (https://tresorit.com/), and Wuala (https://www.wuala.com/) offer cloud storage with zero-knowledge encryption. Check the fine print though, because sharing data with others might mean having your private data decrypted temporarily on the cloud provider server.

5.6 DELETE PRIVATE DATA

Keeping data stored in the cloud private means protecting it in the cloud, in transit to and from cloud storage, and on devices that you use to access the data. In order to completely ensure data confidentiality, you should also remove local copies of private data files and temporary files related to session activity with the cloud storage provider. BleachBit and CCleaner both offer tools to securely delete data on your device.

To securely erase private data from your device, first delete the private data, then use CCleaner (http://www.piriform.com/ccleaner) to delete temporary files and empty the recycle bin. Finally, use CCleaner to securely erase the free space from your drive. Make sure to use the most secure option to make the maximum number of passes over the free space.

BleachBit (http://bleachbit.sourceforge.net/) works similarly to CCleaner to find and remove unnecessary files and erase free space. However, it has a greater focus on privacy and so can find and delete private information stored within many application files without affecting the performance of those applications.

5.7 PERSONAL OR DISTRIBUTED CLOUD STORAGE

If you do not trust the security and privacy policies of commercial cloud storage providers, you can elect to provide your own cloud storage solution. Options include virtual private networks (VPN) and remote access software for virtual network computing (VNC), network attached storage (NAS), private peer-to-peer (P2P) networks, and anonymous P2P networks. Although your concerns about data privacy might motivate you to use one of these options, realize that the burden of security becomes yours. You now have sole responsibility to change default settings, apply the latest security patches, update to the latest versions of software, and review log files for suspicious activity. That said, if you can make these things part of your routine, one of these cloud storage solutions could provide the data privacy you need.

A virtual private network (VPN) or virtual network computing (VNC) software creates a secure network connection between computers. With a VPN or VNC, you and others can access and share private data from anywhere (Figure 5.1).

A VPN or VNC only secures data in transit between computers. Data remains vulnerable at rest on the devices. Furthermore, anyone with the device could have access to private data with an active or auto-login VPN connection. Lastly, companies that offer private VPN services have the ability to log your data, so read their policies regarding this activity. Commercial VPN providers could log and

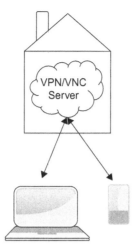

Figure 5.1 Basic VPN/VNC cloud storage architecture.

analyze your data for marketing purposes. Assume free VPN services will almost certainly do this. Remember that if you don't pay for the product then you become the product. Consider strong encryption of your data before transferring it to a VPN-connected directory.

You can run your own VPN/VNC server too. However, if you run it from behind a firewall or without a static IP address, you will have some extra work to do. You will need to configure the firewall to open a port and forward all traffic on this port to your VPN/VNC server. You will likely have a dynamic IP address unless you have purchased a domain name and direct that IP address to your VPN server. Dynamic DNS services like NoIP (http://www.noip.com/) give you a public domain name and keep it synchronized with your dynamic IP address. Finally, you can manually track changes to your VPN server IP address with sites like WhatIsMyIP (http://www.whatismyip.com/), then direct your VPN client to this address.

Microsoft Windows comes with support for VPN. Notable VPN and VNC software include Hamachi (https://secure.logmein.com/), OpenVPN (https://openvpn.net/), RealVNC (http://www.realvnc.com/), TightVNC (http://tightvnc.com/), and UltraVNC (http://www.uvnc.com/). Many more options exist for setting up a VPN to access private data from the Internet, such as SSH. These solutions, while inexpensive to set up, require some IT skills and may not offer the options available in other commercial packages.

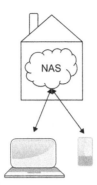

Figure 5.2 Basic NAS cloud storage architecture.

Network attached storage (NAS) devices work as a dedicated Internet accessible file server. Some routers have a USB port where you can attach a storage device and access it from the Internet. In the simplest form, you keep the NAS device in your home or office connected to your network and access it from anywhere with an Internet connection (Figure 5.2).

You can purchase custom NAS devices or you can install NAS software on your own computer. FreeNAS (http://www.freenas.org/) supports encrypted file systems so that only those with the master key can access the file system and the data. Companies like Turnkey Linux (http://www.turnkeylinux.org/fileserver) provide NAS appliances for home and business.

Poorly configured NAS appliances represent a growing data security threat. Search engines like Shodan (https://www.shodan.io/) specifically look for such devices on the Internet. Make sure to change default settings of your NAS and use strong passwords and encryption.

People can create their own cloud to store and share private data by each sharing storage on their own computer (Figure 5.3) or by using a network of anonymous individuals (Figure 5.4). Distributed cloud storage could mean all files get replicated and synchronized across all connected devices, or it could mean storage on each device represents a directory.

Anonymous peer-to-peer (P2P) file sharing networks store your files in cloud space provided by anonymous people or organizations. Of course, this might seem like a step backwards in terms of your data privacy, but it does represent an option if you have confidence in your

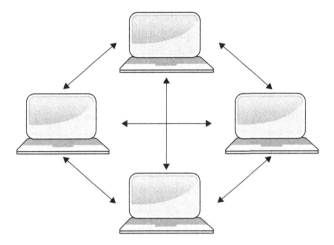

Figure 5.3 Private P2P cloud storage architecture.

Figure 5.4 Anonymous P2P cloud storage architecture.

file encryption. Anonymous P2P file sharing networks do have the advantage of hiding your metadata, such as source and destination IP addresses. You might consider this metadata at least as confidential as the files you want to store, because the IP address can be used to determine your location and the location of the places you visit.

Note that secure P2P networks offering anonymity do so by maintaining a network of thousands of nodes. Such an arrangement might not afford you the right kind of data privacy. Your private data, even encrypted, will exist on and move through nodes of unknown ownership and legal jurisdiction. Unencrypted or easily decrypted private data will exist on many unknown computers within the P2P network. In short, DO NOT equate anonymous with data privacy. If you want data privacy AND anonymity, then you will need to encrypt your data and accept that copies of it might live forever on unknown hosts, accessible to unknown people and organizations.

Some private P2P file sharing tools allow for sharing only among trusted hosts. RetroShare (http://retroshare.sourceforge.net/) calls itself a "secure decentralized communication platform." You can use RetroShare to provide your own private cloud storage solution. RetroShare uses SSL to encrypt data in transit, but you will still need to consider data privacy and security at the endpoints. To use RetroShare, users might have to configure their own firewalls to open a port and forward requests to the computer running RetroShare. Similar P2P file sharing options include GigaTribe (http://www.giga-tribe.com/) and Infinit (https://infinit.io/).

Cubby (https://www.cubby.com/) by LogMeIn offers a secure cloud storage solution that, for a fee, allows users to avoid storing data in the cloud. Instead, files distribute directly between peers. Cubby keeps dynamic DNS and firewall issues transparent to users. Cubby also has security features for revoking permissions and erasing files on devices.

5.8 SECURITY-AS-A-SERVICE

Security-as-a-service (SECaaS or SaaS) provides cloud data security with a cloud service. The SECaaS market continues to grow, especially as more small and medium size companies look to the cloud to reduce costs and improve efficiency. SECaaS allows smaller companies and organizations to outsource cloud security and leverage the infrastructure and expertise of dedicated cloud security experts.

SECaaS creates a layer between applications and cloud data. This layer provides identity and access management (IAM) and allows for single-sign-on (SSO) for all cloud accounts. Applications attempting to access cloud data are redirected to the SECaaS, which authenticates the user and provides a single-sign-on (SSO) for the user to all managed cloud data across all cloud storage providers. Policy-driven key management allows organizations to coordinate data encryption and access. The service manages and distributes keys to authorized users and devices then uses policies to control access to encrypted data.

Key management may include encryption key rotation to coordinate distribution of new keys and decrypting data encrypted with old keys. Full service SECaaS comprises a number of security services, including email virus scanning, encryption, encryption key management, and vulnerability scanning.

Many well-known companies in cloud and computer security have products and services for SECaaS and IAM. Among these include Oracle (http://www.oracle.com/), TrendMicro (http://www.trendmicro.com/), McAfee (http://www.mcafee.com/), and Symantec (http://www.symantec.com/).

5.9 SUMMARY

Throughout this chapter we have discussed tools for individuals and both small and large companies and organizations to protected their cloud data. These tools make it easier to manage cloud data security yourself or augment cloud data security provided to you by others.

Regardless of the tools and services you use to protect your cloud data, your own mind represents one of the best tools for data privacy. Develop and practice these attitudes and habits to maximize the effectiveness of your data privacy tools.

- Resist putting any private data in cloud storage without encrypting it first.
- Use file naming conventions that do not leak metadata about the contents of the file, its creator, or origin.
- Carefully review the security policies of the cloud storage provider before uploading private data. Seek reviews of their security from objective and trusted experts. Look carefully at the details about sharing files and any attached metadata. Know your rights if the cloud storage provider suffers a data breach or loses your data, and what privacy laws apply to your data.
- Secure devices you use to access cloud storage. Apply the latest operating system patches. Update software. Use virus scanners, firewalls, and intrusion detection systems (IDS).
- Only access your cloud data from trusted devices on trusted networks.
- If you must use an untrusted device, keep applications and data on your own USB stick. This will not protect you from keystroke

loggers or possibly having your private data cached on the untrusted hard disk, but it might help keep your data from discovery.

- Limit the number of people with access to your private data. When they no longer need access, revoke their access privileges, change passwords, and/or re-encrypt the data.
- Instruct people with access to your private data about security practices you expect them to follow.
- When accessing your device and cloud storage accounts, beware of shoulder surfers and surveillance cameras that could observe you entering passwords.
- Do not let others use devices that you use to access or cache your private data. The person might see your private data, copy it to an external device, send it as an email attachment, or download malware.
- Take care when keeping local copies of your cloud data. You may want to have local copies of your data so that you can access it regardless of cloud storage provider or network availability, but realize that each copy becomes a vulnerability.
- Applications that access your cloud data should never remain logged in or remember your username and password. Always log out of your cloud storage accounts when not using them. Turn off auto-sync so that even those who successfully log in to your device must still negotiate a separate login to get to your private data. This will protect your private data, but will require you to re-login each time you want to access files stored in the cloud.
- Follow best practices for managing your passwords, including changing your passwords frequently and using strong, random passwords.

REFERENCES

Bletchley Park. Breaking Enigma. [Online] http://www.bletchleypark.org.uk/content/hist/world-wartwo/enigma.rhtm (Last accessed May 2015).

Duckett, C., 2012. Pairing Apache and Google Authenticator. Tech Republic. [Online] 3 September. http://www.techrepublic.com/blog/australian-technology/pairing-apache-and-google-authenticator/ (Last accessed May 2015).

Price, J., 2015. PAM Module Instructions. [Online] 9 March. https://github.com/google/google-authenticator/wiki/PAM-Module-Instructions (Last accessed May 2015).

CHAPTER 6

Best Practices

This chapter highlights best practices for evaluating cloud storage. An example of determining the security and privacy requirement for storing data in the cloud is provided that is based on data type, content, and sensitivity. This is then coupled with user need-to-know to develop a data security policy. A checklist is presented that helps illustrate the kinds of questions that need to be considered when determining security requirements for data cloud storage.

6.1 WHAT ARE BEST PRACTICES?

Best practices are defined as commercial or professional procedures that are accepted or prescribed as being effective most of the time. It can also be considered a heuristic, in that is a rule of thumb that generally succeeds but is not guaranteed to always work in every instance. Given this definition and these caveats, we discuss best practices when considering storing data in the cloud, from a security and privacy perspective.

Best practices, in several important categories, are provided in the form of short statements that identify key cloud storage security concepts. These best practices can be used, along with the checklist in Section 6.2, to evaluate cloud services and their suitability for a specific purpose.

6.1.1 Cloud Provider's Physical Security

- Physical security perimeters should be implemented to safeguard sensitive data and information systems. These can include fences, walls, barriers, guards, gates, electronic surveillance, physical authentication mechanisms, badges, fingerprint scanners, reception desks, and security patrols (CSA, 2015).
- Physical access to information assets and functions by users and support personnel should be controlled and restricted.
- Policies and procedures should be established for maintaining facility security.

- Personnel should be thoroughly vetted and trained in security procedures.
- Facility backup systems should be in place to ensure continuity of operations.

6.1.2 Cloud Provider's Network Security

- The cloud provider should have network security policies that define the security requirements necessary to achieve a specified security posture.
- There should be an architecture diagram that includes hardware and software components that allow the network security policies to be implemented and achieved.
- The architecture should provide the mechanisms to ensure service continuity for the cloud service provider organization. This should include mechanisms to address remediation of failures from the component level to the data center level.
- Customers should be provided with a service level agreement (SLA) that defines the level of service that is guaranteed to the end user of their services. The SLA can specify security, governance, compliance, and liability of the service and service provider.
- The cloud provider should have a policy and plan for responding to security breach incidents. An emergency response team should be identified with the responsibility to address security breaches and implement appropriate remediation measures, as specified in the policy and the incident response plan.

6.1.3 Encryption/Decryption

- Data in motion and data at rest should be encrypted.
- Encryption methods: (1) data-in-motion should use SSL/TLS and (2) data-at-rest should use AES-256. Do not rely on older encryption algorithms, such as Digital Encryption Standard, or nonstandard proprietary formats. While AES-128 is sufficiently robust for most purposes, it may not comply with regulatory mandates, and it may not be as "durable" in the longer term.
- The user organization should control and manage encryption keys.
- Data should be encrypted at the source before being stored in the cloud.
- Data should only be decrypted within the boundaries of the user's organization, not the cloud provider.
- Based on data analysis, create policies that identify which data requires encryption.

- Create policies that define how all encryption/decryption keys will be managed for the entire lifecycle of the data.
- Do not allow cloud providers to have access to keys that protect critical information.
- Do not store encryption keys in the cloud with encrypted data.
- Keys used for encrypting sensitive data should be periodically changed, and data should be re-encrypted with new keys. NIST recommends a *maximum* change period of 2 years, but not a minimum. Obviously changing keys more frequently is more secure than less frequently, but other factors have to be considered, such as the time it takes to decrypt and re-encrypt, data availability during that process, etc. Also it is recommended that encryption keys change when personnel with access to encryption keys leave employment with an organization. There are products on the market and encryption schemes that can facilitate this process. Encryption key change should be defined in the organization's security policy.
- As defined by policy, strong passwords or pass phrases must be used to protect encryption keys.

6.1.4 Authentication and Access Control

- Policies should be created that define the authentication and access control processes.
- Authentication should be based on, as a minimum, user identification and complex password/pass phrase. Passwords should be a minimum of eight characters in length. Longer passwords are more secure and should contain upper and lower case characters, numbers, and special characters. This provides a character set of 95 possible characters. An eight-character password using a character set of 95 has a key space of 95^8, approximately 7×10^{15}, or 7 quadrillion possible passwords. As the key space increases, the time required to perform an brute force attack on a password increases. The addition of two-factor authentication also increases security.
- Employees should be not be given more privileges than what is needed to complete their tasks. This is called the *principle of least privilege*, which refers to restricting users, programs, and processes, to the lowest level of access, read/write, and execution rights necessary to do accomplish their intended work.
- Access logs should be kept and reviewed periodically. Logs should be crosschecked with policy implementation.

6.1.5 Disaster Planning

- Cloud providers should have a disaster plan in place that demonstrates redundancy and failover capabilities to ensure continued service.
- These plans should be reviewed and analyzed by the customer to determine the suitability for maintaining access to your data in the event of a natural or other disaster at the provider's data center(s).
- Customer disaster plans should be updated to include offsite cloud storage.

6.2 GOALS AND QUESTIONS TO ASK ABOUT DATA STORED IN THE CLOUD

In this section, we begin by asking some questions about the data that is to be stored in the cloud. As we illustrate, not all data is created equal – some data is more valuable than other data, and different data have different security and privacy requirements. Also, not everyone needs access to all data. To help us think about data and its value we ask five questions:

- What types of data do we want to store in the cloud?
- What is the value of the data that is being stored in the cloud?
- How sensitive is the data?
- Is some data more sensitive than other data?
- Who should have access to the data and who should not?

6.2.1 Evaluating Data and User Access

In determining the security and privacy requirement for storing data in the cloud, it is a "best practice" to begin by evaluating the type, content, and sensitivity of the data to be stored. Take for example the Acme Widget Company that manufactures an assortment of widgets. They want to move their data from internally controlled servers to an external cloud provider. They have identified four types of data that will be part of their cloud migration: accounting data, user support data, engineering and manufacturing data, and new product R&D data. Each of the four types of data has different security and privacy requirements.

The integrity and confidentiality of the accounting data is of high value in that the company relies on this data to determine the financial well-being, to pay its employees, for future planning, etc. Since this data contains payroll information and employee personally identifiable information (PII), privacy concerns also put this in the sensitive data category. Access to this data must be controlled and restricted.

On the other hand, user support data, while important, does not have the same level of value and sensitivity as the accounting data. It is important for the overall reputation of the company to ensure support for their products, but support information, such as user's manuals, support blogs, support contact information, must be made available to all product owners and anyone interested in their products. This implies that confidentiality is not a concern for product data. Access to this information may be restricted and require user sign-in, or it may be publically available to anyone interested in the products. From a security perspective, the integrity of the information that is made available must be considered. It must be protected from unauthorized modification, which implies that while everyone may have read-access to the data; the ability to modify data content must be strictly controlled. This can be accomplished through user authorization and access restrictions.

Manufacturing and engineering data falls between accounting data and product support data. This data does not have a privacy component, but does contain sensitive information that should be restricted to manufacturing and engineering personnel with a need-to-know.

New product R&D data is more sensitive than manufacturing data because it contains information on future products and is directly tied to the future success of the company. It must be restricted to a smaller subset of employees with a need-to-know. R&D data can also be the target of competitors and certain nation states, attempting to gain competitive advantage. Although R&D data does not have a privacy component, it should be considered high value and sensitive. Access should be tightly controlled and granted on a need-to-know basis.

The other point to be noted is that just because two types of data are highly sensitive, does not mean that if someone can access high-level data of one type that they should also have access to high-level data of another type.

Personnel Versus Data Access				
	Accounting	Support	Manufacturing	R&D
Accounting	X r/w	X read		
Everyone		X read		
Manufacturing		X r/w	X r/w	
R&D		X read	X read	X r/w

The table shows personnel type in the left column and data categories across the top of each of the other columns. The X indicates access to data categories by personnel type. r/w indicates that personnel can read, write, and modify data. As shown in the table, the accounting personnel have both read and write access to the accounting data, but not the other data categories. It also indicates that no one else in the other personnel categories have access to the accounting data. Everyone has access to the support data. This would include visitors from the public internet. Manufacturing personnel are restricted to manufacturing data and may have write access to the support data to make modifications and updates to the support information. R&D personnel are the only ones who can access R&D data, and they have read access to manufacturing and support.

Although this is a simple example of data categorization, it illustrates some of the issues that arise when determining the value of data stored in the cloud. The main point of this section is that not all data requires the same level of protection, and that access to sensitive data should be restricted on a need-to-know basis.

The data that is to be stored in the cloud should be analyzed to determine its value and the sensitivity. In addition, access to the data should also be analyzed to determine who requires access to the data and for what purpose. This forms the foundation for developing data access policies and procedures, which are used to associate data with personnel types/groups and to control data access. This is a primary step in cloud data storage security.

6.3 CLOUD DATA PRIVACY AND SECURITY CHECKLIST

In this section, we present a checklist to help determine the answer to this question: Does the cloud provider and your organization have sufficient policies, procedures, and technology to protect your data?

After each question, the optimal answer is given in parentheses, such as (Y), (N) for yes/no, and (Y/N) meaning there is no correct answer. Some questions require an answer that is an item or a list of items that can only be determined by evaluation of a specific instance. These will be denoted as (List) or (Item).

6.3.1 Cloud Provider – Physical Security
- Is data protected by physical barriers? (Y)
- Is there personnel access control to the facility (badge, pin, retina scan, finger print, etc.)? (Y)
- Are visitors required to be escorted by cleared personnel? (Y)
- Does the cloud provider have backup power? (Y)
- Does the cloud provider have backup cooling systems? (Y)
- Is there 24/7 physical security monitoring? (Y)
- Has the service provider ever had a physical security breach? (N)
- Does anyone other than service provider employees have access to the servers, systems, and data? (N)

6.3.2 Disaster Planning
- Is data stored redundantly? (Y)
- Is data geographically dispersed? (Y)
- Does the cloud provider have failover processes and procedures in place? (Y)
- Is there automatic failover in case of a disk/server/site failure? (Y)
- How often is it tested? (Item)
- What is the guaranteed up time (this should be defined in the SLA)? (Item)
- If a data center has a catastrophic failure, how long will it take to restore access to your data? (Item)

6.3.3 Cloud Provider Personnel
- Are cloud provider personnel required to pass a background check? (Y)
- Are they required to pass a financial stability investigation? (Y)
- Is there a security awareness training program for personnel? (Y)
- Are all employees trained? (Y)

6.3.4 Cloud Provider Network Security
- What policies, procedures, and technology does the cloud provider have in place to ensure data security (firewalls, intrusion detection systems, authentication and access control systems; logging and analysis of: network traffic, authentication, logon/logoff, access, etc.)? (List)
- Does the cloud provider have policies and procedures in place to handle security events? (Y)

- Do they have an emergency response team? (Y)
- Are there remedial procedures in place to address a security incident? (Y)
- Does the cloud provider have redundant connections to the internet? (Y)
- What is the maximum data throughput? (Item)
- What is the current average data throughput? (Item)
- What is the customer's guaranteed data throughput defined in SLA? (Item)

6.3.5 Data in Motion
- Is data in motion between the user and cloud provider encrypted? (Y)
- Is data in motion between cloud provider data centers encrypted? (Y)
- What is the method of encryption? (Item)

6.3.6 Data at Rest
- Is data at rest encrypted? (Y)
- What kind of encryption is used? (Item)
- Who controls the encryption keys? (Item)
- How are keys protected? (Item)
- Where/how are the keys backed up? (Item)
- Are backup copies of encryption keys stored in an offsite location? (Y)
- How are the keys managed? (Item)
- Can multiple keys be created and used to segregate users? (Y)
- Can a master key be created? (Y)
- Can keys be revoked? (Y)

6.3.7 Data Encryption and Decryption
- When is the data encrypted? (Item)
- Where is the data encrypted? (Item)
- When is the data decrypted? (Item)
- Where is the data decrypted? (Item)

6.3.8 File Content Deletion
- When files are deleted is the disk space return to an "available pool" that may be allocated to other customers? (Y/N)
- Is deleted file space securely overwritten to ensure that data content is unrecoverable? (Y)
- When a file is deleted, is it completely deleted from all systems? (Y)

- Is there a retention period for deleted files? (N)
- When media are decommissioned, what are the disposal procedures? (Item)
- How do they ensure erasure of all data? (Item)

6.3.8.1 Incident Response
- Has the cloud provider ever had a data or physical security breach? (Y/N)
- Did they notify their customers of the breach? (Y)
- Does the contract or SLA with the cloud provider require notification of a breach? (Y)

6.3.9 Authentication
- What is the method of user authentication? (Item)

6.3.10 Data Access
- Who has access to your data? (Item)
- Does the cloud storage provider have access to data content? (N)
- Does the cloud provider use your data content for any other purpose except to provide storage? (N)
- Do third parties have access to your data? (N)

6.3.11 Access Control (This Applies to Both Customer and Cloud Service Provider)
- What are the mechanisms that control user access? (List)
- Who controls access? (Item)
- Are access logs kept? (Y)
- Are access logs reviewed? (Y)
- Is there a policy that defines access privileges? (Y)
- Does the policy distinguish between create, read, read/write/modify, and delete? (Y)

6.3.12 Passwords
- Do you have a password policy? (Y)
- How is it implemented? (Item)
- Are there rules in place for password strength? (Y)
- How often are passwords changed? (Item)
- Does the cloud provider have security policies? (Y)
- Are there differences between the cloud provider's security policies and your organization's security policies? (Y/N)

- What are the differences, if any? (List)
- Are different passwords used for cloud storage access and for internal services? (Y)

6.3.13 Legal Jurisdiction and Regulations
- Where will data be stored? (List)
- Is data stored in the United States? (Y/N)
- Is data stored in a foreign country(s)? (Y/N)
- If yes, which country(s)? (List)
- Can you specify in which countries data can be stored and where it cannot? (Y)
- What are the data protection laws in the relevant jurisdiction(s) and what are the security ramifications? (List)
- Where are the backup/redundancy systems located? (List)
- Is the data governed by US federal, state, or foreign government regulation (HIPAA, GLBA, SOX, etc.)? (Y/N)
- Does the cloud provider address compliance issues? (Y)

6.3.14 Third Party Audit
- Has the cloud provider undergone an external security audit? (Y)
- Who performed the audit? (Item)
- When was it performed? (Item)
- What were the results? (Item)
- Are the complete results available for review? (Y)

6.3.15 Other Things to Consider When Storing Data in the Cloud
This section asks questions that should be considered when using cloud storage services. Answers to these questions are subjective and will depend on the actual application and use of cloud storage. They are provided as an aid to begin a conversation about aspects of cloud storage that should be considered.

- What are the risks and benefits of cloud storage to an organization?
- What if the cloud provider goes out of business?
- What if the cloud provider is sold to another company?
- What if a cloud data center is located in a country where there is political or financial turmoil?
- Do you need a backup to the backup provided by a single service provider?

- If you are migrating data to the cloud, how long will it take to do so?
- What are the bandwidth requirements?
- Can the organization and the cloud provider support the upload/download bandwidth requirements?
- Does the cloud provider offer data migration using physical media?
- If you change cloud service providers, does the cloud service provider have procedures in place to facilitate the transfer?
- How long will that process take?
- If the data stored in the cloud is compromised, what are the ramifications to the organization based on the type of data that might be compromised?

6.4 SUMMARY

This chapter highlights best practices for evaluating cloud storage. An example of determining the security and privacy requirement for storing data in the cloud is provided that is based on data type, content, and sensitivity. This is then coupled with user need-to-know to develop a data security policy. A checklist is presented that helps illustrate the kinds of questions that need to be considered when determining security requirements for data cloud storage.

REFERENCE

CSA, 2015. Cloud Security Alliance [Online] Available from: <https://cloudsecurityalliance.org> (accessed March 2015).

CHAPTER 7

The Future of Cloud Data Privacy and Security

Thus far we have covered current problems and solutions related to cloud data security and privacy. In this chapter we look to the future and consider cloud data security in possible brave, new worlds. We first look to the near future and speculate about how current cloud data security and privacy will evolve. We give special consideration to default encryption, two-factor authentication, zero-knowledge encryption, anonymity networks, the monetizing of cloud data security, home clouds, and legal challenges. Next, we look farther into the future with the Internet of Things, quantum physics, and DNA-based data storage devices.

7.1 THE BEST TO EXPECT IN THE NEAR FUTURE

Cloud data storage and services will continue to grow. More people and companies will keep more of their confidential data in the cloud. With more people having more confidential data in the cloud will come a greater awareness of the vulnerability of personal data. This greater awareness of cloud data privacy and security will manifest itself the in following areas:

- Encryption by default
- Two-factor authentication
- Zero-knowledge encryption
- Anonymity networks
- Monetizing security and privacy
- Home clouds
- Security versus safety

7.1.1 Encryption by Default

Google and Apple now encrypt the data that they store on devices by default. Expect default encryption to become standard for cloud storage providers. Note that this encryption applies to data on the device itself and not to data backed up to cloud storage. These providers still have the ability to give the unencrypted data in response to law enforcement requests

(Kravets, 2014). This also means your cloud data remains vulnerable to attackers and malicious insiders with access to the data center servers.

7.1.2 Two-Factor Authentication

Two-factor authentication might not have the success that was anticipated because many perceive it as an inconvenience that requires a second step and the dependency on an additional hardware device. The device associated with the two-factor authentication could get broken, lost, stolen, or left somewhere; all of which mean not having access to cloud data. While backup codes, multiple trusted devices, and applications like Google Authenticator (https://itunes.apple.com/app/google-authenticator) or Authy (https://www.authy.com/) make it possible to remedy these situations, the hardware device requirement and management leaves many looking for easier ways to achieve data security.

7.1.3 Zero-Knowledge Encryption

Zero-knowledge encryption will compete with default encryption for securing cloud data. Recent incidents in the news about governments, companies, and criminals continue to erode the trust people have in cloud storage providers to manage data encryption. Cloud data storage providers will promote zero-knowledge encryption as the only real way to secure personal or corporate data. Companies especially will look to zero-knowledge encryption to protect their data (Vijayan, 2013).

7.1.4 Anonymity Networks

For those seeking to protect their cloud meta-data, anonymity networks like Freenet (https://freenetproject.org), I2P (https://geti2p.net/), and Tor (https://www.torproject.org/) will grow in popularity. These anonymity networks allow for anonymous access to cloud storage. You must still encrypt the stored data, but the anonymity network prevents your provider from tracking your IP address or physical location. Tails (https://tails.boum.org/) provides a live operating system with Tor and other tools for anonymous Internet activity. Tails can be installed on and executed from a USB memory stick, leaving no trace on the host computer once Tails is shutdown and the memory stick is removed. The creators of Tails have the goal of making anonymity online easily accessible to everyone anywhere.

On the negative side, using these anonymity networks to move even encrypted data in and out of the cloud creates the possibility that a rogue node will make a copy of the data and attempt a brute force or cryptographic attack on it. Furthermore, anonymity networks do have vulnerabilities that can expose the identity of users. On the positive side, the hypothetical increase in anonymity of the increasing size of these networks will make them more secure for users, and more difficult for those wanting to monitor your on-line activity.

7.1.5 Monetizing Security and Privacy

We expect to see growth in niche services that provide cloud data privacy. Data security comes at a price and free cloud data storage costs somebody. Cloud storage providers typically use free accounts to build a customer base to attract investors, show advertisements, and sell additional services. These activities, to do well, require user data, hence the need to collect information from user metadata and content. Reputable companies do not use this data maliciously. However, its existence makes it attractive to criminals and authoritarian governments.

Cloud storage providers could seek to increase sales with fee for accounts offering encryption and security compliance, e.g., Safe Harbor or HIPAA. Providers might offer free accounts with large amounts of unencrypted storage, and then encourage users to secure it with encryption for a fee. The assurance of compliance with independent security standards will also draw more businesses into using cloud data storage and services.

Expect to see social networking sites offering no user data collection for a fee. Premium accounts will enable more privacy and security options. Other social networking sites will try different business models to find a niche in the cloud data security and privacy market. The social network site Ello (https://ello.co/) formed as a Public Benefit Corporation with the pledge of not collecting user data for tracking, selling user data, or profiting from advertising. It remains to be seen how successful this for-profit business model will become in the cloud data storage and information sharing markets.

7.1.6 Home Clouds

Network Attached Storage (NAS) devices allow individuals and small businesses especially to have their own private cloud data storage. Security concerns will motivate many to provide their own cloud data storage solutions, both private and commercial. Physical control of both endpoints, devices and storage, does satisfy some security concerns, related to legal issues and insider access. However, it does place the burden of security on the owner of home/private cloud. In addition it does not address data backup and storage location redundancy.

Search engines like Shodan (http://www.shodan.io/) crawl the Internet specifically looking for devices connected to it, including NAS devices. Banners returned by these devices upon connection often reveal or hint at vulnerabilities. A security firm recently developed a proof-of-concept worm that infects and propagates via NAS devices. Cyber criminals have already compromised NAS devices to mine Bitcoins, steal data, and encrypt data to hold for ransom (Constantin, 2014).

7.1.7 Security Versus Safety

Governments concerned about terrorism or mass action will seek greater control over all aspects of cloud data security, from data encryption to metadata anonymity. The increasing use of encryption, both key-managed and zero-knowledge, and anonymity networks may motivate governments to mandate the use of backdoors to bypass cryptographic safeguards, or perhaps even outlaw online anonymity.

Expect governments to continue vilifying the "Dark Net," characterizing it as something used only by criminals and terrorists. The Government Communications Headquarters (GCHQ), part of the British intelligence service, takes the view that technology companies represent terrorist command-and-control infrastructure. Many in GCHG believe this justifies any and all surveillance measures to everyone using these technologies (BBC News, 2014).

Many have characterized the Dark Web as something used by criminals only. In reality, the Dark Web means "By invitation only and no one invited you." This may offend people who don't like to be excluded. Yes, crime happens over encrypted and anonymous Internet traffic. However, crime also happens in the clear, behind closed doors and in secret locations too. In the United States, the government does not have unlimited powers of search and seizure. But many want the legal authority to allow 24/7 tracking and access of all individuals on the Internet. Just because technology makes something easy at scale does not mean we should do it.

Governments will continue to push the agenda that cyber-attacks represent the greatest threat faced by the civilized world, that this justifies unlimited surveillance, and detractors represent threats. In many ways, this concern seems justified. We have more critical infrastructure connected to the Internet with more of its data in cloud storage. Protectors of these systems arguably need whatever advantage they can get to discover and stop cyber-attacks before they do harm. It always comes back to the balance between security versus privacy.

However, asymmetric access to and control of information by governments has not proven a good thing in human history. Knowledge brings power. Concentrating great knowledge and great physical power in an organization with a legal mandate to use it will inevitably result in malicious people working their way into positions of authority within the system and exploiting its power from within.

As a result, oversight will remain a problem with the introduction of any new cloud data storage technology. Intelligence and law enforcement agencies will want to bypass security with laws and backdoors so they can perform their necessary functions. However, people must clearly define what security and anonymity features to bypass, by whom, and by under what circumstances. Otherwise, significant opportunities exist for abuse.

With due process and pro-active oversight, we can balance personal privacy and public safety. Unfortunately, the government of no country has yet mastered this art such that individuals can legally challenge a government related cloud data security issue easily and cost-effectively.

7.2 NEW TECHNOLOGIES AND OLD PROBLEMS

We now take a longer term view of cloud data security. We create new technologies to solve problems. Yet, these new technologies do not so much make the problem go away as they provide a fresh perspective on the old problem. This section highlights three technology trends that will likely provide long-term challenges to cloud data storage privacy and security: the Internet of Things, quantum memory, and DNA-based data storage devices.

7.2.1 Cloud of Things

The Internet of Things (IoT) relates to ubiquitous computing and the pervasiveness of devices connected to the Internet. The sheer number of devices and the volume of data collected create an opportunity for large-scale data analysis that only cloud computing can provide. Hence, we now see the emergence of the Cloud of Things (CoT). The CoT will give effectively unlimited data storage and data processing capabilities to even the simplest devices in the IoT (Aazam et al., 2014).

The number of network-enabled devices continues to grow with devices ranging from home appliances, watches, to automobiles. While Internet connectivity allows these devices to provide useful data to the user, these devices can also make your data available to others, providing information such as location, current activity, activity over time, even your mood, and the ability to correlate this information with your existing profile. With the Internet of Things, we each become "Citizen Sensor."

Your location, sights and sounds around you, your interactions with people and things, and your mood all represents data about you that you might want to keep private and secure. Even when in public, most people would feel uncomfortable with someone following them around and recording everything they did. Your smart device puts this data in the cloud for others to use.

Google Glass allows people to download data about their immediate surroundings and also to capture and upload new information that it and you collect. Images and perhaps other information may include other people. Such devices transform people into data collection tools. Every person with such a device effectively becomes a mobile CCTV camera recording the activities of every person in their view, in addition to recording their own activities and what attracts their attention. Fast facial recognition algorithms and dedicated processors will advance us toward real-time identification and tracking of everyone, connected or not. Imagine advertisers able to access such data, ostensibly collected in public places, who could use this to identify you and track your activities as part of their marketing research. If they only use this information for targeted advertising then it might involve a win-win for both you and the company doing the advertising. On the more sinister side, the existence of this data makes you vulnerable to unknown people with unknown intentions. In addition, this data can have both criminal and civil legal ramifications by providing information on who you associate with, where you were at a specific time, what you were doing, etc. In the extreme, the Frank family in 1942 Nazi Germany would not have gotten to a safe house unobserved.

The variety and number of everyday items able to connect to the Internet will increase. This Internet of Things offers new ways to store new types of data about you in the cloud. You make real-time data about yourself and those around you available in the cloud. At any time, providers, third-party customers of the provider, and hackers can login and download the latest version of your data. Think of it as collaborative cloud data service. You update your life, others read it and profit from it, hopefully without inconveniencing you in the process. What could possibly go awry?

A 2014 Hewlett-Packard report on the Internet of Things (Hewlett-Packard, 2014) found privacy and security issues in most of the devices they tested. They tested a variety of devices such as televisions, thermostats, door locks, and sprinkler systems. Most devices stored data in the cloud. The study found that devices collected personal data not needed for their function, did not require strong passwords, did not use secure network connections, had vulnerable network interfaces, and did not sufficiently protect their software and firmware.

Recently, data watchdog groups found a Russian-based website showing live feeds of webcams from baby monitors (Kelion, 2014). Not changing default passwords, or using weak password protection, either by design or user error, will make webcams and other devices a source of cloud data for hackers and cyber-criminals, as well as put private data at risk.

Researchers in China have now begun looking at the Social Web of Things (Cheng et al., 2014). The Social Web of Things will connect the Internet of Things through a social network interface like Facebook. One day soon you might friend your refrigerator and communicate with it through your social networking accounts using a simple rule-based if-then interface. Such technology will make real-time data about your life available in the cloud. Furthermore, imagine if you do not eat according to approved government guidelines and your refrigerator unfriends you or organizes an intervention by notifying people in your social network.

7.2.2 Future Data Storage

In this book we have discussed the various aspects of cloud storage as it relates to data security and data privacy. We have not focused on the mechanisms that provide the ability to store data and information. Currently most cloud storage providers use magnetic media, mostly in the form of hard drives that use disks coated with a metallic oxide to provide the actual storage mechanism. Some cloud providers are offering solid-state drives, which provide significantly faster access times than magnetic hard drive solutions, as a premium service at an additional cost.

Hard drives were first invented by IBM in the 1950s and were commercially available in 1956. While the basic technology using magnetic media has been improved and miniaturized, the basic technological concept has remained the same: a spinning disk (or cylinder) coated with a ferromagnetic material that is magnetized in one of two directions, which is used to represent a binary "1" or "0." The 1's and 0's are written and read at specific addressable locations on the disk to provide the ability to store data.

Solid state drives on the other hand, use semiconductor chips instead of magnetic media to store data. There are no moving mechanical parts. Binary 1's and 0's are represented using transistors that are switched either on or off. The advantage is that solid state drives have faster access times. Their disadvantage is that they tend to decay over time because of the underlying physics of the transistor and connections tend to build up electrical resistance with repeated erase/write cycles. Currently available solid state devices can deliver up to 50,000 erase/write cycles before this occurs.

As previously pointed out, solid state drives are becoming an option for users of cloud storage, albeit at an additional cost. In the near future solid state drives will likely become more prevalent as the cost of this storage device technology becomes more competitive in price. However, the same security and privacy issues remain despite the underlying technology.

7.2.3 Quantum Memory

One area of research that may impact the future of cloud storage is quantum computing. At universities worldwide, physicists are pushing the envelope using the concepts of quantum physics to store data using the nucleus of atoms. Specifically, at Canada's Simon Fraser University (SFU) researchers have encoded information in the form of quantum bits, called qubits, into the nuclei of phosphorus atoms held in a purified substrate of silicon. They used magnetic field pulses to tilt the spin of the nuclei to "write" qubit memory. Since qubits rely on the spin of nuclei, it is important that these materials are kept near absolute zero, which minimizes noise at the atomic level and increases the stability of qubits. What makes the SFU research interesting is that they were able to maintain qubit stability at room temperature for 39 minutes and were able to manipulate qubits as the temperature climbed and fell back toward absolute zero (ACM, 2013). While this may not sound like much, it was a significant achievement in the path toward quantum memory and quantum computing.

Qubits have a number of interesting properties that researchers are investigating. In a quantum system, a qubit is stored in a superposition state where it can represent both 1 and 0 at the same time. This property, as researchers note, enables qubits to perform multiple calculations simultaneously.

Another property that is intriguing in the application of quantum computing to cloud security is the concept of quantum entanglement. Entanglement is a property that allows a set of qubits to express a high degree of correlation even if separated by distance. The implications of this property is that if a set of entangled qubits are in different locations, a change in value of a qubit at one location will also be reflected in the qubit value in another location – without any physical connection. (Actually, if the qubit in one location has a value, or spin, interpreted as 1, then the value of its entangled qubit will be 0, and vice versa, which can easily be accounted for in its interpretation). In a research paper entitled *Unconditional Quantum Teleportation between Distant Solid-State Quantum Bites* (Pfaff et al., 2014), researchers demonstrate unconditional teleportation of arbitrary quantum states between the spin of diamond-based qubits separated by 3 meters.

In the future, quantum communications and quantum networks may provide a new modus operandi to securely transmit and store data in cloud structures without the need for transport encryption. Many research hurdles are left to conquer. And as usual, this new technology will inevitably provide new opportunities and a new set of security challenges.

7.2.4 The Future of Storage Technology – DNA

We now take a look at the cutting edge of research in storage technology and consider what the more distant future of storage technology has in "store." Specifically we look at one possible future that brings together biology and computer science to provide massive storage capabilities that can store data for hundreds of thousands or even millions of years. The new approach has some built-in security features that are unavailable in current technology, but as with most new technology, it comes with its own set of new security concerns.

Every living creature on earth shares one thing in common: they contain the molecular instructions for life called deoxyribonucleic acid or DNA. Encoded within DNA are the instructions for building, maintaining, and replicating an organism. The information in DNA is stored as a code made up of four chemical bases: adenine (A), guanine (G), cytosine (C), and thymine (T). Human DNA consists of a set of about 3 billion of these bases. The order, or sequence, of these bases determines the information available for building an organism, similar to the way in which letters of the alphabet appear in a specific order to form words, sentences, paragraphs, and chapters (NIH, 2015).

DNA bases pair with each other in sets of two: A with T and C with G, to form units called base pairs. Together, a base, sugar, and phosphate are called a nucleotide. Nucleotides are arranged in two long strands that form a spiral called a double helix, as shown below.

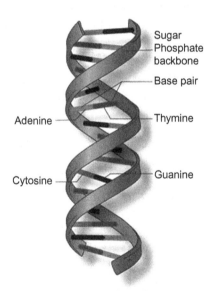

Structure of the double helix (Courtesy of the National Human Genome Research Institute's Talking Glossary http://www.genome.gov/glossary/).

The structure of the double helix is somewhat like a ladder, with the base pairs forming the ladder's rungs and the sugar and phosphate molecules forming the vertical sidepieces of the ladder (NIH, 2015).

From biology we know it is the order of the bases along a single strand that determines the genetic code. Bases are read in sets of three to form the instruction, or code, (in biology they are called codons) that determine which amino acid (building block) to use. A sequence of amino acids, called a gene, are linked together to form a protein by reading the nucleotides along a DNA strand. Certain three-letter nucleotide codons specify start and stop positions within the DNA strand, much like the computer programming language construct BEGIN/END, or the bit sequences found in communication protocols, or end-of-file markers (Winburn, 2015).

7.2.5 Biology to Computer Science

In the simplest case we could use the A-T base pair to represent binary 0 and G-C to represent binary 1. Using this encoding and keeping with biological constructs, reading a sequence of three nucleotides at a time we could represent 2^3 binary values (0−7 decimal) per read; reading 32 sets of 3 nucleotides would result in 96 bits, or 12 bytes of data. For example if we look at the DNA diagram we see that the first three base pairs (starting from the top) are C-G, T-A, and G-C, which using our encoding scheme would represent 010.

Current research in this area has used different encoding and representational schemes. Church, Gao, and Kosuri, in their paper "Next-Generation Digital Information Storage in DNA," calculate that a single-strand of DNA can store 5.49 petabits per cubic millimeter. One petabit is equal to 1000 terabits, or 10^{15} bits. Church's experiments showed that the total writing, amplification, and reading process resulted in 10 bit errors out of 5.27 megabits (Church et al., 2012). Goldman, at the European Bioinformatics Institute, used a different encoding scheme with built-in error correction and was able to write and read 5.2 megabits with 100% accuracy. Using this method, 90 petabytes of data could be stored in 41 grams of DNA (Nature, 2013). Others have theorized that 1 gram of DNA is capable of storing 455 exabytes (10^{18} bytes). Since all of the information that exists in the world today is estimated to be fewer than 10,000 exabytes, we have the potential of storing all of the world's data in less than a cup of DNA (Frey, 2015).

Still, there are many problems to be resolved to bring this technology into general use. There are issues with both reading and writing

DNA data. With present-day biological processes and techniques there are constraints imposed on both reading and writing DNA data. There are also timing issues that indicate that DNA using current processes would be excellent for long-term data that is stored but seldom read, such as archived satellite data from the Hubble telescope project, data generated by the Hadron Collider experiments, or government records and other information residing in the National Archive.

DNA can remain stable and usable for thousands of years, as evidenced by DNA from a 60,000-year-old wooly mammoth and DNA from a 700,000-year-old horse (Lee, 2013). If DNA is dried and protected from oxygen, water, and heat it can remain stable indefinitely.

Another interesting quality of DNA as a storage mechanism is that in biological settings, it replicates exact copies of itself (mostly). There is the possibility of genetic mutations. The ability to replicate could be used for data backup and versioning.

7.2.6 DNA Storage and Security

DNA could provide a new form of cryptography. A, T, G, and C bases could be paired with 1's and 0's using an algorithmic approach that would scramble the assignment of values; or one strand of DNA might act as a set of indices into another strand to provide address encryption that is needed to reassemble the original data. Many possibilities exist, such as threshold encryption where several strands of DNA from different "organisms" would be required to reconstruct the original data.

Using such an encryption process would make it subject to legal restrictions such as the International Traffic in Arms Regulations (ITAR) and the Export Administration Regulations (EAR), which are export control regulations run by the US government. Imagine the difficulty in the enforcement of these regulations as produce, such as apples or rice, is shipped from one country to another; or people travel from place to place.

Much of the research in DNA storage uses synthetic DNA, which relies on a biological process to create artificial DNA. This process does not require using preexisting DNA sequences from nature. Using synthetic DNA is thought to be safer for experimentation and thus is able to avoid guidelines and regulations on DNA experiments. The National Institute of Health guidelines specify that, "If the synthetic DNA segment is not expressed in vivo as a biologically active polynucleotide or polypeptide product, it is exempt from the NIH Guidelines." Church and others have stated that long DNA fragments are unlikely to replicate on their own or encode anything biologically active. Cells tend to expel DNA that is not their own. However, if placed in the wild, they could get incorporated into a living organism where they have no natural predators and nothing to prevent them from spreading.

Also of concern, is that as information is transformed from the binary 1's and 0's of the digital world into the A, T, G, and C of the biological world, what does the resulting DNA code for in biological organisms? For example, does the photo of your mother in JPG format translate into an infectious biological virus? Or does reading a biological strand of DNA translate into an infectious computer virus? The question, from a security perspective, is what is the meaning of these seemingly random 1's and 0's in biological terms and in computing terms? Clearly there are many interesting research problems to consider and to resolve.

Then there is the ethical issue of whether or not we should be manipulating and experimenting with the fundamental mechanisms of life in this way. Answers to those questions will be answered by the theologians, philosophers, ethicists, and scientists.

7.2.7 The Cloud – Data, Information, Questions

Throughout this book, we have discussed the concept of storing information in the cloud, but we have not defined information, as a concept. Physicist Eliyahu Goldratt has a simple and elegant definition: "Information is the answer to the question asked." Data can provide a diverse array of information if we ask the right question. The cloud contains the data; it contains some information; the future will be determined by the questions that we ask.

In one possible future, using DNA, we may become the storage device – where all of us, together, become the cloud. Then the problem will be, what questions should we ask? Sound vaguely familiar?

REFERENCES

Aazam, M., Hung, P., Huh, N., 2014. Cloud of Things: Integrating Internet of Things with Cloud Computing and the Issues Involved. Proceedings of International Bhurban Conference on Applied Sciences & Technology. Islamabad, Pakistan, January 14-18, 2014. [Online] Available from: http://www.staffs.ac.uk/assets/harvard_referencing_examples_tcm44-39847.pdf   (accessed April 2015).

ACM, 2013. Quantum Memory 'World Record' Smashed [Online] Available from: http://cacm. acm.org/news/169870-quantum-memory-world-record-smashed/fulltext (accessed May 2015).

BBC News, 2014. GCHQ's Robert Hannigan says tech firms 'in denial' on extremism. [Online] 4 November. Available from: http://www.bbc.com/news/uk-29891285 (accessed April 2015).

Cheng, C., Zhang, C., Qiu, X., Yang Ji, Y., 2014. The Social Web of Things (SWoT) – Structuring an Integrated Social Network for Human, Things and Services. J. Comput. 9 (2), [Online] Available from: http://www.jcomputers.us/vol9/jcp0902-13.pdf (accessed April 2015).

Church, G.M., Gao, Y., Kosuri, S., 2012. Next-generation digital information storage in DNA. Science 337 (6102), 1628 [Online] Available from: http://www.sciencemag.org/cgi/content/full/ science.1226355/DC1 (accessed April 2015).

Constantin, L., 2014. Researcher creates proof-of-concept worm for network-attached storage devices. PC World. [Online] 20 October. Available from: http://www.pcworld.com/article/ 2836112/researcher-creates-proofofconcept-worm-for-networkattached-storage-devices.html (accessed April 2015).

Frey, T., 2015. The Great Cow Epiphany and the Six Immutable Laws of Information. [Online] 26 February. Available from: http://www.futuristspeaker.com/2015/02 (accessed April 2015).

Hewlett-Packard, 2014. Internet of Things Research Study. [Online] Available from: http:// h20195.www2.hp.com/V2/GetDocument.aspx?docname=4AA5-4759ENW (accessed April 2015).

Kelion, L., 2014. Breached webcam and baby monitor site flagged by watchdogs. BBC News. [Online] 21 November. Avaibable from: http://www.bbc.com/news/technology-30121159 (accessed April 2015).

Kravets, D., 2014. Apple, Google default cell-phone encryption "concerns" FBI director. [Online] 25 September. Available from: http://arstechnica.com/tech-policy/2014/09/apple-google-default-cell-phone-encryption-concerns-fbi-director/ (accessed April 2015).

Lee, J.J., 2013. World's Oldest Genome Sequenced From 700,000-Year-Old Horse DNA. National Geographic. [Online] 27 June. Available from: http://news.nationalgeographic.com/ news/2013/06/130626-ancient-dna-oldest-sequenced-horse-paleontology-science   (accessed   April 2015).

Nature, 2013. Synthetic double-helix faithfully stores Shakespeare's sonnets. [Online] Available from: http://www.nature.com/news/synthetic-double-helix-faithfully-stores-shakespeare-s-sonnets-1.12279 (accessed April 2015).

NIH, 2015. Genetics Home Reference. [Online] Available from: http://ghr.nlm.nih.gov/handbook/ basics/dna (accessed April 2015).

Pfaff, Hensen, Bernien, 2014. Unconditional quantum teleportation between distant solid-state quantum bits [Online] Available from: http://www.sciencemag.org/content/345/6196/532.abstract (accessed May 2015).

Vijayan, J., 2013. Cloud computing 2014: Moving to a zero-trust security model. [Online] 31 December. Available from: http://www.computerworld.com/s/article/9244959/Cloud_computing_ 2014_Moving_to_a_zero_trust_security_model (accessed April 2015).

Winburn, B.M., 2015. Conversation on DNA structure and the relationship to binary sequences. Transcription 3133, 7.

.

Printed in the United States
By Bookmasters